Research and Development Portfolio Management

Michael Popp

Research and Development Portfolio Management

Learning From Company Practices and Experiences

VDM Verlag Dr. Müller

Impressum/Imprint (nur für Deutschland/ only for Germany)
Bibliografische Information der Deutschen Nationalbibliothek: Die Deutsche Nationalbibliothek verzeichnet diese Publikation in der Deutschen Nationalbibliografie; detaillierte bibliografische Daten sind im Internet über http://dnb.d-nb.de abrufbar.
 Alle in diesem Buch genannten Marken und Produktnamen unterliegen warenzeichen-, marken- oder patentrechtlichem Schutz bzw. sind Warenzeichen oder eingetragene Warenzeichen der jeweiligen Inhaber. Die Wiedergabe von Marken, Produktnamen, Gebrauchsnamen, Handelsnamen, Warenbezeichnungen u.s.w. in diesem Werk berechtigt auch ohne besondere Kennzeichnung nicht zu der Annahme, dass solche Namen im Sinne der Warenzeichen- und Markenschutzgesetzgebung als frei zu betrachten wären und daher von jedermann benutzt werden dürften.

Coverbild: www.purestockx.com

Verlag: VDM Verlag Dr. Müller Aktiengesellschaft & Co. KG
Dudweiler Landstr. 99, 66123 Saarbrücken, Deutschland
Telefon +49 681 9100-698, Telefax +49 681 9100-988, Email: info@vdm-verlag.de

Herstellung in Deutschland:
Schaltungsdienst Lange o.H.G., Berlin
Books on Demand GmbH, Norderstedt
Reha GmbH, Saarbrücken
Amazon Distribution GmbH, Leipzig
ISBN: 978-3-639-18159-3

Imprint (only for USA, GB)
Bibliographic information published by the Deutsche Nationalbibliothek: The Deutsche Nationalbibliothek lists this publication in the Deutsche Nationalbibliografie; detailed bibliographic data are available in the Internet at http://dnb.d-nb.de .
Any brand names and product names mentioned in this book are subject to trademark, brand or patent protection and are trademarks or registered trademarks of their respective holders. The use of brand names, product names, common names, trade names, product descriptions etc. even without a particular marking in this works is in no way to be construed to mean that such names may be regarded as unrestricted in respect of trademark and brand protection legislation and could thus be used by anyone.

Cover image: www.purestockx.com

Publisher:
VDM Verlag Dr. Müller Aktiengesellschaft & Co. KG
Dudweiler Landstr. 99, 66123 Saarbrücken, Germany
Phone +49 681 9100-698, Fax +49 681 9100-988, Email: info@vdm-publishing.com

Copyright © 2009 by the author and VDM Verlag Dr. Müller Aktiengesellschaft & Co. KG and licensors
All rights reserved. Saarbrücken 2009

Printed in the U.S.A.
Printed in the U.K. by (see last page)
ISBN: 978-3-639-18159-3

Preface

This book is based on my master's thesis I have finished 2007. So that time, I wrote my thesis, with a topic somewhere between business and engineering, while living and doing interviews with companies in Sweden. How did this come about?

The idea for the topic had come to my mind during a mountain hike at home in Austria – ideas do not necessarily emerge at an office desk or an R&D laboratory. I had desired to work on a practical topic. And I had set my heart on addressing both business issues and technology issues as I studied both business administration and electrical engineering, even tough it was the thesis for business administration only. With neither much knowledge of practice nor impressions of literature, I had come up with the management of the bunch of technology projects at a company, somewhere in the middle of the way up to the mountain summit. After reviewing some of the literature, I realised it was an important topic indeed. Today, I'd even like to consider R&D management as the supreme discipline in combing business and technology.

And why in Sweden? This idea neither emerged at home at the desk, but in Finland. During my exchange semester, I studied at Svenska handelshögskolan, the Swedish-speaking business university in Helsinki. So I started learning Swedish language and loving Northern landscape and wilderness. Then Sweden sounded pretty obvious, just the next country with Northern landscape and wilderness and – even more – Swedish language.

Yet the basic idea had emerged long before at home in Austria indeed. I wanted to write my thesis abroad, in English, touching business and technology, and gaining company practice.

Still, I was alone with my idea. I needed a company and an advisor. At a business university, it might happen that you will find dozens of departments loving money, but never daring to touch R&D projects. Yet one department does. I don't know why I had never got in contact with them before. However, one colleague there kindly agreed to supervise my thesis.

Merely one ingredient missing, the company. Originally, I had intended to write my thesis at only one and for one company, to gain especially intensive practice. While still struggling to find a company which would appreciate a student sitting at their site and writing a complete master's thesis about them, my advisor suggested to better have a look at more than one company by doing a number of interviews, since this would give a broader spectrum. If he would have known that this would end up in comparing truck firms with pharmacy firms and paper firms with radioactive waste storage laboratories, he might have reconsidered!

So not only one ingredient missing, but many. But phoning companies and asking them for interviews was funny. In some companies, I almost found the right person on their internet site. In some companies, the switch board was reluctant to connect me to any person unless I knew the name. In some companies, I asked at the switch board for R&D management, were still curiously waiting for how I would come wrong this time, until I realised my direct hit as the person answered "Yes, I am responsible for R&D in Sweden".

Then everything was in place. I had my student home situated pretty in the nature just outside Stockholm, with a large construction site in front of my window which created a stimulating busy atmosphere when I was sitting alone at home working. I had my advisor whom I could write e-mails or phone in order to ask him repeatedly for an extension of the deadline and specific questions about my work. And most importantly, eventually I had all my company contacts who kindly allowed me to visit them and ask them why they don't do it as I had read in the books.

I sincerely like to thank all my interview partners for being interested in my topic, for their truly interesting information and their stories from practice, for their time, and for their hospitality. And I like to thank my advisor for his valuable inputs and his patience, starting when iteratively forming a proper thesis proposal and never ending when extending the deadline for delivering my work several times.

This work not only aims to be a scientific master's thesis, but also a practically valuable reading for practitioners. The decision whether I have succeeded will be up to my readers.

Michael Popp

Stockholm, October 2007
and Munich, July 2009

Content

1 Introduction 13
   1.1 About the topic 13
   1.2 Overview of existing literature and emergence of need for
       further research 13
   1.3 Aims of this thesis 16
   1.4 Research procedure and creation of results 17
   1.5 Some definitions 19

2 Approaches in the current literature 21
   2.1 Historical overview 21
   2.2 Process flow and essence of portfolio management 22
   2.3 Strategy and portfolio goals 26
   2.4 Tools for project evaluation 27
       2.4.1 Financial values 28
       2.4.2 Scoring, checklists, and rankings 29
       2.4.3 Diagrams for categorisation 31
       2.4.4 Strategic buckets 35
       2.4.5 Feature targets 37
       2.4.6 Project selection models 37
       2.4.7 Making decisions or only supporting decisions 43
       2.4.8 Usability for portfolio goals 44
   2.5 Portfolio review and project selection process 45
       2.5.1 Purpose and modality 45
       2.5.2 Preparations 46
       2.5.3 Discussion and preliminary project decisions 47
       2.5.4 Final adjustments and decisions 48
   2.6 Project gate process and handling of individual projects 49
       2.6.1 Purpose and modality 49
       2.6.2 Typical process 50
       2.6.3 Two decision steps at each gate 54
       2.6.4 Adjustments for various project types 55
   2.7 Combining the portfolio review and the project gates 58

2.8 Allocating resources 60
2.9 Success and influence factors 63
   2.9.1 Overview of studies 63
   2.9.2 Some concrete factors 66
2.10 Some opinions and thoughts 70

3 Insights from practice 73
3.1 Strategy and portfolio goals 73
3.2 Tools for project evaluation 79
   3.2.1 Financial value 79
   3.2.2 Scoring, checklists, and rankings 82
   3.2.3 Diagrams for categorisation 84
   3.2.4 Strategic buckets 86
   3.2.5 Feature targets 88
   3.2.6 Standardised playing cards 91
   3.2.7 Using tools for decisions 92
3.3 Strategic planning, portfolio review process, and decisions there 97
   3.3.1 Modality of happenings 97
   3.3.2 Extent of project evaluation 98
   3.3.3 Main purpose of the review and project selection 100
   3.3.4 Conclusion 101
3.4 Project gate process and handling of individual projects 102
   3.4.1 Purpose and modality 102
   3.4.2 Considering the whole portfolio 104
   3.4.3 Pre-studies and project selection 105
   3.4.4 Conclusion 105
3.5 Various levels of sophistication in portfolio management 106
3.6 Starting with the ideas or with the markets 108
3.7 Company organisation, standardisation, and local and central decisions 114
   3.7.1 Organisation of the portfolio into different business and R&D units 115
   3.7.2 Standardisation 117
   3.7.3 Decisions locally or centrally 118
   3.7.4 Conclusion 119
3.8 Allocating resources 120
3.9 Differentiation between product portfolio management and project portfolio management 121
3.10 Common challenges and problems 122

4 Notable overall company methods 129
    4.1 Filling up intended levels of future revenues and R&D costs 129
    4.2 Sophisticated strategic buckets 132
    4.3 Assessing the project value in research 135

5 Conclusions 138

6 Literature 143

1 Introduction

1.1 About the topic

R&D portfolio management is about doing the right R&D projects and allocating the available R&D resources in the most effective way. It means to initiate new R&D projects in the company's project portfolio, to set priorities among them, to review the portfolio periodically and to cancel poor ongoing projects. For a technology company that is reliant on its innovations, these tasks are not just administrative ones but are the basis for implementing the company's strategy.

1.2 Overview of existing literature and emergence of need for further research

Literature

A large part of the literature attempts to explore the factors in portfolio management approaches which make companies successful, so to reveal the success factors and best practice.[1] Determining the factors correlating with success is interesting for theory as well as for practice where these findings can be utilised. These factors are reviewed in Chapter 2.9. Apart from listing

---

[1] Cooper/Kleinschmidt (1986); Cooper/Kleinschmidt (1995a); Cooper/Kleinschmidt (1995b); Cooper/Kleinschmidt (1996); Cooper/Edgett/Kleinschmidt (1997a); Cooper/Edgett/Kleinschmidt (1997b); Cooper/Edgett/Kleinschmidt (1998); Cooper (1999); Cooper/Edgett/Kleinschmidt (1999); Cooper/Edgett/Kleinschmidt (2000); Cooper/Edgett/Kleinschmidt (2001); Cooper/Edgett/Kleinschmidt (2004a); Cooper/Edgett/Kleinschmidt (2004b); Cooper/Edgett//Kleinschmidt (2004c); Cooper (2005); Cormican/O'Sullivan (2004); Davidson/Clamen/Karol (1999); Griffin (1997); Matheson/Matheson/Menke (1994); McQuater/Peters/Dale/Spring/Rogerson/Rooney (1998); Menke (1997a); Menke (1997b); Page (1993); Poolton/Barclay (1998); Song/Parry (1996); Yap/Souder (1994); Zirger/Maidique (1990).

success factors, many of this best practice articles describe such portfolio practices in terms of portfolio goals, processes, and instruments. These, broadly, are treated across the literature in Chapter 2. Somewhat the opposite view is taken by the literature exploring what the major problems are.[2] Moreover, some articles do not attempt to reveal new success factors but rather survey the host of existing literature and try to structure and evaluate the current state.[3]

The other group of articles which is concerned with success factors does not focus on overall portfolio management but on single projects and tries to identify the factors which, on the one hand, help a project succeed and which, on the other hand, enable an early evaluation whether it will be a success or better should be abandoned.[4] These factors are considered in Chapter 2.4.6.

Two papers have developed frameworks for the process of portfolio management, which fulfil some basic propositions and then can be flexibly filled with methods and instruments to apply.[5] These are considered introductory in Chapter 2.2.

Some articles attempt to classify different project types and, consequently, suggest different management methods for them within the same portfolio.[6] This is considered in Chapter 2.6.4.

There are some other articles which do not address R&D portfolio management directly, yet highlight closely related topics. First, some papers especially focus on the organisational and people aspect of running several interdependent projects in a company; so they consider multi-project

---

[2] Elonen/Artto (2003).
[3] Brown/Eisenhardt (1995); Dooley/Subra/Anderson (2002); Kahn/Barczak/Moss (2006); Montoya-Weiss/Calantone (1994).
[4] Cook-Davies (2002).
[5] Archer/Ghasemzadeh (1999); De Maio/Verganti/Corso (1994).
[6] Dewar/Dutton (1986); Ettlie/Bridges/O'Keefe (1984); Dvir/Lipovetsky/Shenhar/Tishler (1998); Payne/Turner (1999); Shenhar (1993); Shenhar/Dvir (1995); Shenhar (2001).

situations.[7] The idea is to "coordinate projects to gain benefits that would not be possible if the projects were managed independently".[8] Second, many articles investigate project management of only one project. Yet these ones addressing highly complex projects with many multi-functional sub-tasks are also interesting from the portfolio perspective.[9] Third, some articles are basically about keeping the company creative and free for ideas and thereby fostering innovations.[10] Fourth, some articles are about the company's core competences in technology and marketing and about exploiting them for several projects and products.[11] Fifth, some articles emphasise the link between R&D and marketing and product planning.[12]

Generally, the literature is pretty focused on practice, trying to suggest processes and guidelines for coping with portfolio management in the practice of an organisation.

Need for further research

So far literature has given less consideration to questions of how companies are faring with their rules, processes, and instruments for portfolio management and what their reasons are for having chosen to do so as they do. Yet these questions seem relevant for developing even more practice-orientated theories that do not only recommend which instruments and processes generally to implement but also how to cope with all the arising difficulties when working with them and how to adopt it to various individual company cases.

---

[7] Bart (1988); Danilovic/Sandkull (2005); Dietrich/Lehtonen (2005); Engwall (2003); Eskerod (1996); Ferns (1991); Frumerman/Cicero/Baetens (1987a); Frumerman/Cicero/Baetens (1987b); Gray (1996); Gray/Bamford (1999); Lycett/Rassau/Danson (2004);Payne (1995); Pellegrinelli (1997); Platje/Seidel (1993); Platje/Seidel/Wadman (1994); Scheinberg/Stretton (1994); Thiry (2002); Turner/Speiser (1992); Van Der Merwe (1997); Van Der Merwe (2002); Wiley/Deckro/Jackson Jr. (1998); Yang/Sum (1997).
[8] Ferns (1991), p. 155
[9] Griffin/Page (1993); Söderlund (2002).
[10] Amabile (1998); Bellmann/Schaffer (2001); Keegan/Turner (2002).
[11] Danneels/Kleinschmidt (2001); Meyer/Tertzakian/Utterback (1997); Nobeoka/Cusumano (1997).
[12] Griffin/Hauser (1996); Hart/Tzokas/Saren (1999); Moenaert/Souder (1990); Souder/Song (1997); Wheelwright/Sasser Jr. (1989).

For answering these questions, instead of sending questionnaires to many companies, it seems more useful to individually investigate companies and their R&D portfolio management in more detail. Indeed, some studies investigate only few companies, but these in more detail, and attempt to answer such questions.[13] Yet they are only few articles, partly many years old.

This thesis explores a few companies qualitatively and thereby attempts, first, to reveal practical challenges when applying all the suggested portfolio management methods, second, to provide new insights and ideas from practice and, third, to reveal the reasons why companies in fact have chosen to do so as they do.

1.3 Aims of this thesis

This thesis has two major aims.
1. It shall state the processes and instruments of literature about how to manage a technical R&D projects portfolio, thereby reviewing the state of the literature as well as giving a compact manual on this management topic.
2. It shall provide a qualitative description of company practices with these processes and instruments. This is, first, how they manage their portfolio, second, which positive and negative experiences they have with it, and third, their reasons for their choices why they do it as they do. This comprises especially the processes and decisions when reviewing the portfolio and when evaluating single projects for project selection, the instruments used there, and the portfolio goals strived for.

---

[13] Eskerod (1996); Fricke/Shenhar (2000); Frumerman/Cicero/Baetens (1987a); Krogh/Prager/Sorensen/Tomlinson (1988); Rzasa/Faulkner/Sousa (1990).

Though, according to Nobelius, an isolated project portfolio is obsolete and nowadays R&D is a network of collaborations[14], a company's own project portfolio still does matter and is this work's major topic.

Though computer programmes are of course an important mean of consequent implementation in company practice, this work does not consider computer programmes but only the processes and methods in themselves.

1.4 Research procedure and creation of results

Research procedure and structure of results

The first research aim of this thesis, presenting the state of the literature as described in Chapter 1.3, shall be fulfilled in Chapter 2 by exploring and structuring the current literature on this topic. This part is the basis on which to build the new insights of this work. Yet it should be practice-orientated enough for being a support for companies on their portfolio management.

For gaining practical experience and fulfilling the second research aim, stating the companies' way of working, I have done 15 interviews in industry companies in Sweden. Managers, responsible for portfolio management, were interviewed in a personal meeting. The interviews were conducted according to a questionnaire which was broadly created according to the structure of the theory and with concern for covering all the issues needed for meeting the research aim. Each interview was recorded using a voice recorder and then transcribed to text.

While coming along with the interviews, I realised that no company works according to the structure of my questions. Moreover, I got a better understanding of the topic and could better adapt the conversation to the specific company case. Hence, I attempted to cover all my questions by getting the big picture of each company's situation rather than by sticking to the prepared questions. And of course, an interview run was fairly much

---

[14] Nobelius (2004), p. 370.

shaped by my interview partner's flow and manner of talking about his or her company.

The insights and possibly new knowledge are presented in two chapters. Chapter 3 describes the ways in which the companies work, structured according to the topics similar to Chapter 2. Both well-known and new methods are described. Moreover, as far as discovered, the reasons are given why these methods are applied and preferred by the companies. The insights are reflected whether already stated by literature. Finally, apart from the thematic structure, Chapter 4 describes the interesting overall approaches of three companies. So these two chapters shall fulfil the work's second research aim.

Quality of results

The fairly small number of companies does not allow decisive conclusions. The wide spread of companies across different industry branches on the one hand improves the broad scope of insights, while one the other hand even further reduces the number of companies with comparable conditions. Therefore, the yield of this work is seen as insights and practical evidences which bear relevance to at least some company cases. Company managers might take them as an advice as far as applicable to their businesses. Science might take my hypotheses and refine my other insights into hypotheses for testing them on a greater sample.

Interviewed companies

Figure 1.1 lists all interviewed companies with industry branch and number of interviews. All interviews were done in Sweden at company departments located there.

Company	Branch	Number of interviews
ABB	Power and automation	1
AstraZeneca	Pharmaceuticals	1
Atlas Copco	Mining equipment	1
Electrolux	Appliances	1
Ericsson	Telecommunication	3
Infineon	Semiconductors	1
Saab	Aviation	1
Sandvik	Steel technology	1
SCA	Paper	1
Scania	Automotive	1
Svensk Kärnbränslehantering SKB	Radioactive waste storage	1
Volvo	Automotive	2

Figure 1.1 Interviewed companies

1.5 Some definitions

Literature uses the terms new product development (NPD) as well as research & development (R&D). This work intends to consider research, product development, and any related kind of projects and uses the term R&D as an overall term. Articles cited in this work are considered in the same way, regardless whether they talk about NPD or R&D, unless they specify their scope more closely.[15]

The terms instruments and tools are used synonymously is this work. And they do not mean a computer programme. Instruments and tools, in this work, mean what is described in the Chapters 2.4 and 3.2. These are methods for doing evaluations, prioritisations and so on of the projects, regardless whether done on a computer, on paper or somewhere else.

The terms milestones and gates are used synonymously in this work.

When talking about resources, generally all kinds are meant, as people, money, and equipment.

---

[15] So too handled in Cooper/Edgett/Kleinschmidt (1998), p. 33, note 1.

A classical funnel system refers, figuratively, to a funnel, having a wide end and a narrow end. The company gathers many ideas from several sources, starting at the wide funnel end. As they proceed, within the funnel, they are sorted out; only the best ideas go on. Finally, a few ideas remain, at the narrow funnel end.

2 Approaches in the current literature

2.1 Historical overview

Nobelius provides an historical overview how R&D management has developed from around the year 1950 until today and groups this period into five generations. The basic tendency is that R&D management has become more open for and linked with its environment. At the beginning, R&D was an almost isolated, technology-driven ivory tower in a company. At the third generation from mid-1970s to mid-1980s, a portfolio view emerged, moving away from considering projects only separately; and links to business and strategy were considered. Nowadays in the fifth generation, R&D is a network of collaborations with customers, competitors, suppliers, and distributors; technology investments are heavy and need to be shared. Competition is global and technology changes quickly. Product development is more strongly separated from research as speed for market launches is essential.[16]

Souder/Mandakovic state that before 1950, R&D was only a modest part of an economy and hardly managed. Only then, organisations began to create more project ideas than they actually could run, therefore starting to think about project selection methods.[17]

In 1997, Griffin looks back 15 to 20 years. She finds that R&D developed rather slowly and evolutionary, not revolutionary. Companies need to change to prevent falling behind, yet change is slow because R&D is so complex, as she assumes. Over the course of these 15 to 20 years, R&D changed from a sequential, functional undertaking to a multi-functional one.

---

[16] Nobelius (2004), p. 370.
[17] Souder/Mandakovic (1986), p. 37.

And R&D's organisation has become more complex. She concludes that R&D has become slightly more efficient and faster, yet success rates have stayed the same.[18]

2.2 Process flow and essence of portfolio management

Process flow

Figure 2.1 shows the flow of a typical portfolio management process. First of all, the strategy has to be decided, defining the strategic focus and maybe a total budget. Then new project ideas come in from any source. They are evaluated, in a first step independently of the whole portfolio. And a decision how to proceed is made. This includes considering the strategy and current market conditions, and can take some instruments for support. When knowing about each idea or project, one step further, the whole portfolio is reviewed. Again this is done with strategy and market conditions in mind and the help of instruments. Additionally the resource situation for the whole portfolio is considered. For instance, an idea endorsed in the single evaluation could get cancelled in the portfolio review because others are even better and resources are too scarce for all. And differently from the single project evaluation, project dependencies and interactions are taken into account. So the portfolio review ends up with portfolio decisions. In the next step, eventually, the everyday work on the project has to be done. From time to time, the ongoing projects will pass the loop again. Each single project will be evaluated at its milestone reviews, as well as the whole portfolio at the portfolio reviews. Finally the project work has created a new product (which may be approved in a last milestone, not shown in the graph).

---

[18] Griffin (1997), p. 450.

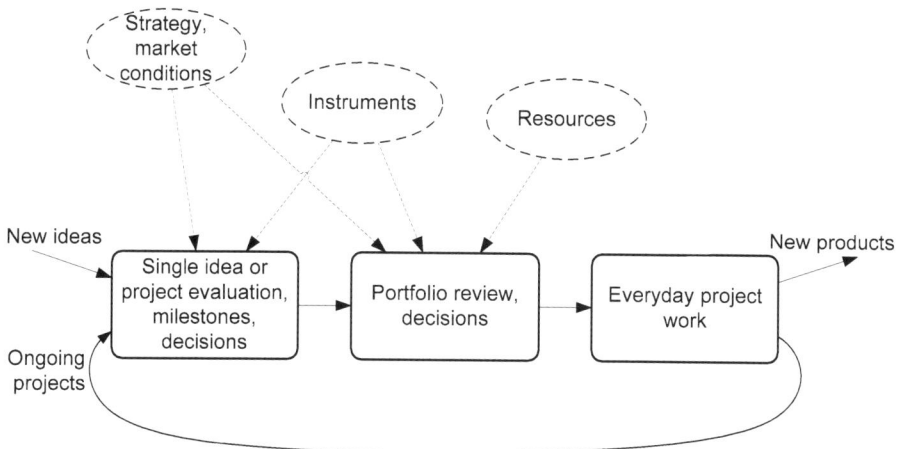

Figure 2.1 Process flow of portfolio management[19]

The introduced process flow is based on both Archer/Ghasemzadeh and De Maio/Verganti/Corso.[20] Archer/Ghasemzadeh explicitly separate two steps in what I have combined under the name portfolio review. As their first step, they basically decide about the optimal portfolio selection, usually with the help of instruments. At the second step, managers are given the option to adjust this selection and go back to the first step to re-evaluate their adjustments.[21] De Maio/Verganti/Corso emphasise the classification and, if necessary, re-classification of projects in this process as every manager tries to categorise new problems based on his past experience. Further, they in fact do not mention strategy, but evaluate projects in terms of relevance, risk, and critical resource requirements.[22] However, having in common in both models, the evaluation of an individual project is done before the portfolio review; and ongoing projects are periodically re-evaluated as individual projects, which is the essence of a milestone process.

---

[19] Modified and combined from Archer/Ghasemzadeh (1999), p. 211 and De Maio/Verganti/Corso (1994), p. 183.
[20] Archer/Ghasemzadeh (1999); De Maio/Verganti/Corso (1994).
[21] Archer/Ghasemzadeh (1999), p. 211.
[22] De Maio/Verganti/Corso (1994), p. 183.

Cooper/Edgett/Kleinschmidt point out that both the milestone process and the portfolio review are important components of the whole portfolio management, as the former ensures a deep project analysis while the latter provides a holistic view. Hence, both stand side by side, are driven by strategy, and interact with each other.[23]

Tuominen/Piippo/Ichimura/Matsumoto describe a flow model from a different perspective. They state three main forces that will direct the innovation process: goals and strategy, customer's needs and requirements, and technological opportunities. Further, the competitive situation has an impact. Taking these four input factors, a product innovation management system has to ensure that the development work fulfils four output criteria: right products and characteristics, right time to develop and launch, right amount of investment, and right, effective implementation.[24]

To conclude, all author's suggestions indeed are compatible with each other, yet highlight somewhat different aspects.

Essence of portfolio management

What portfolio management, basically, is about has become clear when looking at its process flow above. Additionally giving a straight definition by Cooper/Edgett/Kleinschmidt, R&D portfolio management is "a dynamic decision process, whereby a business's list of active new product and R&D projects is constantly updated and revised. In this process, new projects are evaluated, selected and prioritised; existing projects may be accelerated, killed or de-prioritised; and resources are allocated and reallocated to the active projects. The portfolio decisions process is characterised by uncertain and changing information, dynamic opportunities, multiple goals and strategic considerations, interdependence among projects, and multiple decision makers and locations."[25]

---

[23] Cooper (2005), p. 137.
[24] Tuominen/Piippo/Ichimura/Matsumoto (1999).
[25] Cooper/Edgett/Kleinschmidt (1997a), p. 16.

Along with this definition, there are many challenges and tricky issues surrounding portfolio management decisions:

- Project and product management is about future events and opportunities. So a lot of the information needed for decisions is presently still highly uncertain. This also means that the result of a decision might become apparent only after some years; hence it often is difficult to judge a decision's quality for the time being.[26]
- Often there are interrelated multiple selection criteria and, further, interrelated resources.[27]
- Qualitative factors as strategy alignment are – apart from uncertainty – difficult to measure and to assess.[28]
- The decision environment is pretty dynamic. The status and prospects of both the market and the projects themselves might change as new information becomes available.[29]
- The projects in the portfolio are at different stages of their development cycle, thus have different information quality. Yet they need to be compared against each other as all of them compete for the same resources.[30]

Cooper/Edgett/Kleinschmidt suggest that portfolio management is separated into a strategic level and a tactical level. The strategic level comprises decisions about broad resource allocation to different product areas, see Chapter 2.4.4 for strategic buckets. Further, the creation of product roadmaps and a rough total spending on R&D in the company are strategic decisions. On the tactical level, periodic portfolio reviews and project gate processes are conducted, considering and deciding about specific projects.[31]

---

[26] Cooper/Edgett/Kleinschmidt (1997a), p. 17; Matheson/Menke (1994), p. 39; Patterson (1998), p. 390; Schmidt/Freeland (1992), p. 189.
[27] Schmidt/Freeland (1992), p. 189.
[28] Schmidt/Freeland (1992), p. 189.
[29] Cooper/Edgett/Kleinschmidt (1997a), p. 17.
[30] Cooper/Edgett/Kleinschmidt (1997a), p. 17.
[31] Cooper (2005), p. 136.

2.3 Strategy and portfolio goals

Cooper/Edgett/Kleinschmidt state some goals for the project portfolio. In earlier articles, they name three goals.[32]

1. **Ensuring strategic alignment.** All projects should support the strategy and be crucial components of it. The projects' segmentation according business areas and markets should reflect the strategic segmentation and the strategic focus.
2. **Maximising the value of the portfolio.** For the given spending level, portfolio value should be maximised. This value can be determined in different ways, for instance likelihood of success, return on investment, or estimated sales value.
3. **Seeking the right balance of projects.** Balance can be achieved in terms of long-term and short-term projects, high-risk and low-risk projects, various markets, technologies, product categories, and project types (product improvements, new products, fundamental research).

In later works they have added two more goals, thus having a set of five goals now.[33]

4. **Ensuring a sufficient portfolio output for reaching the product innovation goals.** For example, if twenty percent of sales next years should come from new products, or if you want to address a certain market with plenty of new products, the current projects in the portfolio need to support this. So forecasting the current projects yield must match the future market goals.
5. **Matching the number of projects with the available resources.** This goal mainly aims at not having too many projects in the portfolio. If there are more projects than actually resources available, projects get stuck in a queue and take a long time to market.

---

[32] Cooper/Edgett/Kleinschmidt (1997a), p. 19.
[33] Cooper (2005), p. 114.

Indeed, the new goal of sufficient portfolio output makes sense, as Chapter 3.1 will show from company practice. Yet the match between projects and resources, though important, might be about avoiding the mistake of starting too many projects as an important side condition rather than being a true goal giving direction.

The goal to maximise the portfolio's value aims at the efficiency of the portfolio. It requires that the projects are good enough. Contrary, the strategic goal and the balance goal rather aim at the effectiveness of the portfolio. They require that the projects are the right ones. Both perspectives are important for a good portfolio.[34]

While aligning the portfolio to strategy and gaining some desired profit are goals that are straightforward to set, even though maybe tough to fulfil, the goal of the right portfolio balance might be ambiguous. Once the balance of the current portfolio is evaluated, there is often lack of a should-be balance to compare it against.[35]

As I have found in literature, Cooper/Edgett/Kleinschmidt are the only ones who state such portfolio goals. Other authors just state broadly strategy as what the portfolio needs to strive for.[36] Yet there is no contradiction since issues like financial goals and balance between certain business areas, indeed, can be part of the strategy. Cooper/Edgett/Kleinschmidt yet present it in a more structured, detailed way.

2.4 Tools for project evaluation

Here the instrument categories and instruments of the literature are introduced.

---

[34] Based on Cooper/Edgett/Kleinschmidt (1997a), p. 23.
[35] Cooper/Edgett/Kleinschmidt (1997a), p. 27.
[36] Archer/Ghasemzadeh (1999); Englund/Graham (1999), p. 52; Hall/Nauda (1990).

2.4.1 Financial values

This kind of instrument calculates a financial result or value of a project, basically considering costs, earnings, and mostly also risk. The net present value (NPV), return on investment (ROI), payback period (BBP), and capital asset pricing model (CAPM) are possible examples.[37]

Figure 2.2 depicts the principle for the NPV. After having invested the development costs, the project might technically fail or succeed and continue, depending on the probability of technical success. After it was launched and has succeeded commercially too, the earnings start to come in. So the NPV, according to the formula in the figure, is given by the costs and earnings, weighted by the probabilities that they will occur.[38]

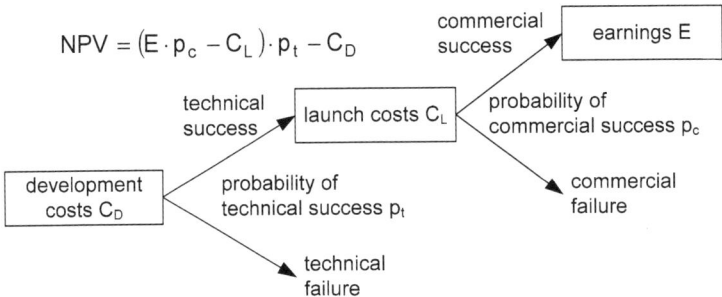

Figure 2.2 Principle of net present value (NPV) calculation[39]

Advantages

- Talking in financial terms is a widely used language since all companies have some kind of financial accounting.[40]
- The instrument considers not only the earnings but also the expenses. It strives for allocating the resources to where they are used most efficiently.[41]

---
[37] Archer/Ghasemzadeh (1999), p. 209; Kahn/Fiorino (1992).
[38] Cooper/Edgett/Kleinschmidt (1997a), p. 20.
[39] Cooper/Edgett/Kleinschmidt (1997a), p. 20.
[40] De Maio/Verganti/Corso (1994), p. 183.
[41] Cooper/Edgett/Kleinschmidt (1997a), p. 20.

- Money amounts can be discounted to today, depreciating projects that are years away from launch.[42]
- When using a decision tree as in Figure 2.2, the model recognises that some costs do not incur in case of earlier cancellation. For example, in case of technical failure, at least the launch costs are saved.[43]

Disadvantages

- The major weakness is the dependence on its data. You need estimates of future earnings, launch costs, development costs and success probabilities. These are often unreliable or not available early in the project life.[44] Even worse is that the result is a cosy number that wrongly implies precision.
- More venturesome projects get punished by lower success probabilities respectively need higher earnings for getting the same result values.[45]

2.4.2 Scoring, checklists, and rankings

Scoring is a simple tool for evaluating projects. At least in principle. A set of criteria is rated for each project and summed up to a project score, obtaining an overall prioritisation list by ranking the individual project scores. However, as this simple result often does not reflect which truly would be the best projects for the company, many authors have suggested adjustments. They use a better formula than just adding up, do adaptations depending on the current project stage, and take past project experience into account. It's somewhat arbitrary what to call just an improved scoring tool and what a whole project selection model. Hence, this chapter describes the basic tool of scoring, while Chapter 2.4.6 contains anything more enhanced.

---

[42] Cooper/Edgett/Kleinschmidt (1997a), p. 20.
[43] Cooper/Edgett/Kleinschmidt (1997a), p. 20.
[44] Cooper/Edgett/Kleinschmidt (1997a), p. 20.
[45] Cooper/Edgett/Kleinschmidt (1997a), p. 20; De Maio/Verganti/Corso (1994), p. 184.

• Strategic fit and importance
  • Alignment of project with business strategy
  • Importance of project to the strategy
  • Impact on the business
• Product and competitive advantage
  • Product delivers unique user benefits
  • Product offers the user excellent value for the money
  • Competitive causes for product
  • Positive user feedback on product concept (concept test results)
• Market attractiveness
  • Market size
  • Market growth and future potential
  • Margins earned by companies in this market
  • Intensity of competition
	• Core competencies leverage
	  • Project leverages the company's core competencies and strengths in technology, production, operation, marketing, and distribution
	• Technical feasibility
	  • Size of technical gap
	  • Familiarity of technology to our business
	  • Newness and maturity of technology
	  • Technical complexity
	  • Technical results by now
	• Financial reward versus risk
	  • Size of financial opportunity
	  • Financial return
	  • Certainty of financial estimates
	  • Level of risks and company's ability to address them

Figure 2.3 Example criteria for scoring[46]

So scoring is based on a list of criteria on which each project is measured. For instance, a criterion can be rated within an area from 1 to 5, with definitions what these values mean. Further the criteria can be multiplied by different weighting factors. Then the sum of all criteria ratings of a project is the score of this project.[47]

Checklists are quite similar. But the criteria are questions that are rated only with yes or no. Again a project result can be calculated by counting the number of questions answered with yes.[48]

The key preparation is to develop a specific set of criteria that reflects the company's needs. A typical scoring set could use criteria as shown in Figure 2.3.

The projects can be ranked according to their scores, resulting in a prioritisation list. Further, a minimum score can be defined that must be passed by each project in an initial screening, otherwise it is refused.[49] As

---
[46] Cooper (2005), p. 144
[47] Cooper/Edgett/Kleinschmidt (1997a), p. 23.
[48] Cooper (2005), p. 154.
[49] Cooper/Edgett/Kleinschmidt (1997a), p. 22.

each project's score is calculated independently, scoring is appropriate when interdependency between the projects is low, so one project does not depend on another project's outcomes.[50]

Advantages

- Scoring has some rigor due to its numerical results, yet does not impose too much mathematical complexity.[51]
- Scoring can take nearly everything into account, also non-quantitative criteria by creating an evaluation scale.[52]
- Scoring does not need financial data, often hardly available at early project stages.[53]

Disadvantages

- As for the financial instruments, the scoring numbers imply a precision that does not exist, since many criterion ratings are just estimations and quite subjective.[54]
- At least for a basic model that considers only the merits but no resources, efficient resource allocation is not evaluated. It might happen that larger projects tend to get higher scores due to higher impact, yet require even more resources.[55]

2.4.3 Diagrams for categorisation

Creativity can lead to many kinds of diagrams. For portfolio management, two types appear notably interesting and common: pie charts, and matrix charts for categorisation along the two axes. The former can be used for displaying any kind of share as technologies in the portfolio or R&D

---

[50] Henriksen/Traynor (1999), p. 162.
[51] Henriksen/Traynor (1999), p. 162.
[52] Henriksen/Traynor (1999), p. 162.
[53] Henriksen/Traynor (1999), p. 162.
[54] Cooper/Edgett/Kleinschmidt (1997a), p. 23; De Maio/Verganti/Corso (1994), p. 184.
[55] Cooper/Edgett/Kleinschmidt (1997a), p. 23.

spending on product lines. The latter which is more special should be depicted here.

They are named matrix chart[56], portfolio grid[57], or bubble diagram because the projects are drawn as circles (bubbles).[58] Many various attributes can be drawn on the two axes, categorising the projects along them. Figure 2.4 shows an example for such a diagram. The vertical axis measures the probability of technical success, thus evaluates the technical difficulty to succeed in developing a certain project. The horizontal axis gives the commercial potential of the projects, so this is the reason why to execute the project. These two dimensions appear to be a quite common and important as "the secret to successful R&D management is understanding the critical relationship between the probability of success and the value of a project given its success."[59] Then the projects are plotted on the positions accordingly. Four quadrants arise that might be given the following illustrative names.

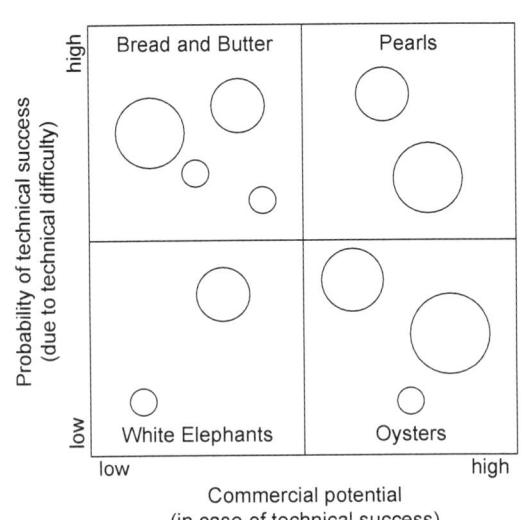

Figure 2.4 Matrix diagram[60]

- Bread-and-Butter projects bear a high probability of technical success, but a low commercial value. Improvements of existing products are typically here. "You need bread-and-butter projects to maintain or

---

[56] Archer/Ghasemzadeh (1999), p. 211.
[57] Matheson/Menke (1994), p. 41.
[58] Cooper/Edgett/Kleinschmidt (1997a), p. 24.
[59] Matheson/Menke (1994), p. 38.
[60] Matheson/Menke (1994), p. 41.

improve near-term performance, but you can't build your future on them."[61]

- White Elephants are technically difficult and gain low commercial value, for example technical complex projects addressing market opportunities that are too small to justify the time and expense they would require. These projects should be avoided respectively cancelled. Their name comes from the legend that the King of Siam gave white elephants to his disagreeable courtiers. Because white elephants were considered holy and could not be disposed of, their upkeep often caused financial ruin.[62]
- Oysters are technically high-challenging projects with a high commercial potential, for instance scientific research. These are long-term projects, designing the future. Work on them needs patience and time and might still fail, but in case of success high reward is near.[63]
- Pearls are the best projects one can have – technically easy to complete, high commercial potential. Typically, this project state is reached only after years of effort.[64]

Many projects move from one quadrant to another during their life cycle. So most R&D efforts start out as either Bread-and-Butter projects or Oysters projects.[65] And "it takes many Oysters to produce a Pearl."[66] So a company should run a number of Oyster projects at the same time. It is part of the business that a few of them will fail and will never become Pearls as long as one of them grows to a Pearl. But it is important to find out as early as possible which ones will fail and therefore must be cancelled. And White Elephants may have once been Oysters that have developed too slowly.[67] It is important to keep the balance between Bread-and-Butter projects for earning

---

[61] Matheson/Menke (1994), p. 40.
[62] Matheson/Menke (1994), p. 41.
[63] Matheson/Menke (1994), p. 41.
[64] Matheson/Menke (1994), p. 41.
[65] Matheson/Menke (1994), p. 41.
[66] Matheson/Menke (1994), p. 41.
[67] Matheson/Menke (1994), p. 42.

the short-term profit and Oyster projects for preparing long-term innovations.

In addition to the project position, more information can be depicted by the size, colour and pattern of a project circle. For instance, the size, or more precisely the area, can show the project's estimated sales potential or its annual R&D expenses, colour and pattern the product line and whether it is in time.[68]

Matrix diagrams can also be used for considering resources. Plotting the project bubbles size, so the area, according to money or people required by the project, you should not let the sum of all project areas exceed your totally available resources.[69]

It is often difficult to produce reliable evaluations where to place a project along the axes. One option is to draw an ellipse for each project, signifying the uncertainty of the evaluations. For each axis, an optimistic and a pessimistic estimation are created, drawing the ellipse according to this range.[70]

Wheelwright/Clark find two other measures on the axes most useful; they suggest the degree of change in the product and the degree of change in the production process. The greater any change along either dimension, the more resources will be needed by this project.[71]

Advantages

- The graphic is a convenient and appealing way of presenting the information.

Disadvantages

- Again as for the other tools, it might be difficult to make reliable evaluations where to place a project along the axes. Yet leastwise

---

[68] Cooper/Edgett/Kleinschmidt (1997a), p. 25.
[69] Cooper/Edgett/Kleinschmidt (1997a), p. 25.
[70] Cooper/Edgett/Kleinschmidt (1997a), p. 25.
[71] Wheelwright/Clark (1992), p. 73.

bubble diagrams don't give the impression of so much precision as numerical instruments do.[72]

- Diagrams only display some information; they do not propose any decision. Even though company decisions are hardly bound to the instruments, it is still helpful to obtain, for instance, a ranking list which only needs to be adjusted. For diagrams, contrary, the way from the instrument result to the final decision is much longer.[73]

2.4.4 Strategic buckets

This is a top-down method that starts with a stated business strategy. Implementing the strategy requires spending money on projects. Hence according to the strategy, you have to decide how to allocate the R&D spending across several different project areas. So you allocate the money into different buckets, hence its name. For instance, a product line, that is especially focused by the strategy, thus will get assigned more resources. These buckets can be defined in terms of product lines, project types (product improvement, new products, cost reduction), markets, technologies, geography, or whatever else seems useful in a certain case.[74]

Current and proposed project ideas are classified into these buckets. Eventually, the total R&D spending of the projects within each bucket should match with what was previously decided to spend on this bucket. As a further refinement, the projects within each bucket can be prioritised and selected up to the bucket's R&D spending level.[75]

Englund/Graham suggest to organise the portfolio into categories, basically depending on the newness, as this will make the project decisions easier. A company will learn over time about finding the best mix.[76]

---

[72] Cooper/Edgett/Kleinschmidt (1997a), p. 27.
[73] Cooper/Edgett/Kleinschmidt (1997a), p. 27.
[74] Cooper/Edgett/Kleinschmidt (1997b), p. 44.
[75] Cooper/Edgett/Kleinschmidt (1997b), p. 45.
[76] Englund/Graham (1999), p. 55.

Advantages

- Strategic buckets firmly link the R&D spending to business strategy, making the portfolio mirroring the business strategy.[77]
- The ranking of projects is done separately within each bucket. The projects there are probably more similar, thus easier to compare, and are fewer. And within each bucket, a scoring and prioritising instrument can be developed that best fits this bucket's project type. So it's not necessary to deploy one universal scoring tool for all different project types.[78]
- Englund/Graham argue that, as companies need to deliver a broad solution to their customers, they seldom have the choice between project categories – they need to do them all, often resulting in too many projects. Strategic buckets enable to invest in each project category, but limit the size of each. Then the company works in all categories, yet will choose the best projects within each category.[79]

Disadvantages

- Splitting resources to buckets without consideration of specific projects may appear hypothetical.[80]
- The advantage of encapsulating projects can also be seen as a disadvantage because not really all projects are compared against each other. So there is the argument that resource spending really should be determined by the projects' merits, not by artificial money buckets. For instance, if all product-improvement projects are superior to any new-product project, no new-product project ought to be initiated and all resources ought to be spent on product-improvement.[81]

---

[77] Cooper/Edgett/Kleinschmidt (1997b), p. 45.
[78] Cooper/Edgett/Kleinschmidt (1997b), p. 46.
[79] Englund/Graham (1999), p. 55.
[80] Cooper/Edgett/Kleinschmidt (1997b), p. 46.
[81] Cooper/Edgett/Kleinschmidt (1997b), p. 49.

2.4.5 Feature targets

This instrument basically is about determining a number of project features that should be achieved, these are the targets to achieve. Then each feature has one or more projects linked that will strive for reaching this desired feature position. This instrument seems hardly known in the literature. I have found it being mentioned only by Rzasa/Faulkner/Sousa[82], there called influence diagram. Company practice reveals a much more sophisticated version in Chapter 3.2.5.

2.4.6 Project selection models

These models partly are extensions of the instruments named above. Especially many of them appear as extended versions of scoring by reckoning a project index from several input factors. Here different ideas of various authors are introduced briefly.

Scoring for different project types

Balachandra/Friar observe that, for evaluating a project, the various criteria have different importance depending on the project type and the market. Figure 2.5 shows their suggestion for criteria importance depending on this project context. There, three parameters of project context as well as three groups of criteria are stated.[83]

Scoring for different stages in the project lifecycle

These approaches intend not to calculate a project score at the project start for selection only, but to calculate and update a score along its lifecycle. Thereby they consider new factors and provide some kind of performance score.

Pillai/Joshi/Rao develop such a tool for calculating a project performance. The considered factors are shown in Figure 2.6. These need to

---

[82] Rzasa/Faulkner/Sousa (1990), p. 29.
[83] Balachandra/Friar (1997), p. 282.

be rated. Then a mathematical function considers all factors of the current and the previous project stages, but of course not the yet unknown future stages, and calculates a performance index. These resulting indexes can be used for a project ranking, especially also for projects in different stages.[84]

Project context			Criterion importance		
Innovation	Technology	Market	Market	Technology	Organisation
Incremental	Low	Existing	Very important	Less important	Very important
Incremental	Low	New	Very important	Less important	Very important
Incremental	High	Existing	Very important	Very important	Important
Incremental	High	New	Important	Very important	Important
Radical	Low	Existing	Important	Important	Important
Radical	Low	New	Less important	Important	Important
Radical	High	Existing	Important	Very important	Important
Radical	High	New	Less important	Very important	Very important

Figure 2.5 Importance of criteria depending on the project context[85]

Current stage	Relevant factors
Initial screening and project selection	• Expected project benefits • Risk, not being able to deliver these benefits • Project category, thus basically more or less important
Development and testing	• Deviations in time, cost and progress • Effective project management, ability to control these deviations
Launch, production, marketing and sales, product support	• Ability to meet production requirements • Cost effectiveness, thereby competitiveness • Ability to win customer commitment and orders

Figure 2.6 Relevant performance factors in each project stage[86]

---
[84] Pillai/Joshi/Rao (2002).
[85] Balachandra/Friar (1997), p. 284.
[86] Pillai/Joshi/Rao (2002), p. 175 and 170.

Kumar/Persaud/Kumar develop a model for supporting the decision of whether to continue or to cancel at each project stage.[87] Basically, it is a scoring instrument which takes some factors into account and results in a score telling the project success likelihood. By regression analysis of past project data, they have determined for each project stage which factors there have a significant relation to final project success or failure and thus are relevant to consider in that specific project stage. Now when applying in a certain project stage, each relevant factor needs to be evaluated by a number; these values are fed into a certain function; the result is a probability of project success. Yet even apart from the calculation approach, their revealed factors relevant for each stage appear interesting, given in Figure 2.7.

Current or just finished stage	Relevant factors
Initial screening	• Project fits for the company's goals and products
Detailed technical and market assessment	• Science and technology available • Project supported by other relevant persons in the company • Truly new usage possibilities for customers • Technical capability adequate to project complexity
Development and testing	• Development process runs efficiently, without too much unexpected setbacks in time, costs, resources, and additional adjustments; smooth internal communication • Technical characteristics fit consumer, marketing, and sales-margin expectations
Marketing and sales preparations, pre-production, initial market testing	• Technical capability adequate to project complexity • Marketing efforts

Figure 2.7 Relevant success factors in each project stage[88]

---

[87] Kumar/Persaud/Kumar (1996).
[88] Kumar/Persaud/Kumar (1996), p. 280 and 277.

39

Formula for adding up the criteria

Henriksen/Traynor have developed an advanced scoring model.[89] It uses a special formula that calculates the result from the input criteria, considering each criterion adequately. It considers criteria of project merit as strategic relevance, risk, reasonableness given the available resources, basic research return, applied research return, and business return, as well as required resources by a cost criterion.

The outcome consists of two numbers for each project: first, the project's merit, and second, its value which considers merits and costs.

The merit criteria can be added up or can be multiplied. Henriksen/Traynor find that some criteria depend on each other; these should be added up but not multiplied. For instance, projects with potential for high return mostly bear high risk. Let us assume a scale from 1 (bad) to 5 (good). A high-return high-risk project would get 5 for return and 1 for risk, resulting in a partial score of 5 x 1 = 5 by multiplying. The same score for a low-return low-risk project, 1 x 5 = 5. Yet the average project always would win, having 3 x 3 = 9. Contrary when adding the criteria, these three projects would get the same scores, 5 + 1 = 6, 1 + 5 = 6, and 3 + 3 = 6, which is basically desirable. On the other hand for criteria that contribute independently to the project quality, they should be multiplied in order to emphasise each criterion's importance and to avoid a high ranking of a project faring extremely poor in any criterion.[90]

NewProd, comparing criteria with experience

Cooper has developed a computer-based scoring instrument, where each project can be rated on a set of criteria. Now the special feature is a database. These rating profiles are compared with the profiles of a large number of past projects in the database. By knowing the eventual performance of these database projects, the likelihood for success, project

---

[89] Henriksen/Traynor (1999).
[90] Henriksen/Traynor (1999), p. 164.

strengths and weaknesses and so on are reckoned for the projects currently under evaluation.[91]

Criteria with the analytical hierarchy process

The analytical hierarchy process is a scoring and decision instrument developed by Saaty.[92] First, a set of criteria is created. Second, each criterion is compared pair wise against each other criterion, setting a score of their relative importance. Third, for each criterion, each possible project is compared pair wise against each other project, setting a score on which project fulfils this criterion better. Finally, usually by a computer, the project scores and thus a ranking are calculated. Further, the instrument can maintain the decision quality by recognising some inconsistencies, for instance when for a certain criterion project A was evaluated better than project B, B better than C, yet in turn C better than A.[93]

Calantone/Di Benedetto/Schmidt evaluate this model in practical use for the screening of new project proposals and conclude it is well suited.[94] They argue that, especially with many alternatives, the decision is a pretty complex one. Since humans cannot consider so much information in mind at one time, decisions are rather taken on a subset of information, unless they use such decision support systems.[95]

Project cancellation by deteriorated criteria

Bard/Balachandra/Kaufmann develop a model for deciding about project cancellation by regularly observing whether some project conditions have deteriorated. There are four must-meet criteria; if one of them fails, the project should be cancelled. Then there are 14 further criteria considering the environment, the project, and the organisation. At each review, a project score is calculated by adding one point for each criterion that has not got

---

[91] Cooper (1992).
[92] Saaty (1980).
[93] Wikipedia (2007).
[94] Calantone/Di Benedetto/Schmidt (1999).
[95] Calantone/Di Benedetto/Schmidt (1999), p. 69.

worse since the last review. A score of more than eight, thus six or less deteriorated criteria, should indicate a high probability of success.[96]

Important deliverables of different project types

Shenhar/Dvir/Levy/Maltz find that the deliverables and goals to achieve by a project ought to be considered dependent on the project type. A project could be measured along four goals: efficiency in terms of time and budget; impact for the customer and satisfied specifications; business success for the own company in terms of profit, sales, gained market share, improvement of internal processes; and future preparations as new technologies, new ideas, new skills, and competences. Apparently, these goals are sorted ascending with a more long-term perspective. And projects too get classified according to their time horizon, whereas a longer time horizon mostly goes along with higher technological uncertainty. Accordingly, the goals by which to measure a project should be weighted. For a short-term project, efficiency may be the most important goal; it won't cause a technological impact anyway. On the other hand, for a long-term project, business success and preparing the future may weight much more than getting it finished a little cheaper and faster.[97]

Optimisation models

There are some models available which calculate an optimal portfolio by mathematical optimisation.[98] For instance, they start with the individual project values, consider project interactions, constraints, and multiple objectives, and try to calculate an optimised projects portfolio.[99] Yet they are not considered further in this work since they both appear to have less

---

[96] Bard/Balachandra/Kaufmann (1988).
[97] Shenhar/Dvir/Levy/Maltz (2001).
[98] Archer/Ghasemzadeh (1999), p. 210; Bard/Balachandra/Kaufmann (1988); De Maio/Verganti/Corso (1994), p. 184; Granot/Zuckerman (1991); Graves/Ringuest/Case (2000); Jackson (1983); Ringuest/Graves/Case (1999); Schmidt/Freeland (1992), p. 189; Souder (1973), p. 907.
[99] Archer/Ghasemzadeh (1999), p. 210; De Maio/Verganti/Corso (1994), p. 184.

practical relevance[100] and were not used by any company interviewed for this thesis.

Further models

Schmidt/Freeland provide a classification of project selection models into three categories and present a comprehensive list for each.[101] Also Baker gives a review about such models.[102]

2.4.7 Making decisions or only supporting decisions

Instruments can be categorised into decisions-making ones and decision-supporting, only information-displaying ones.[103] The former give a result that could be immediately translated into a decision. For example the resulting prioritisation list from scoring could be considered as decision-making, simply doing all the projects starting from the top of the list as far as resources are available. Of course some adjustments of this ranking might be recommendable, but not necessary in principle. Contrary, matrix diagrams for instance only show a kind of balance. Their information supports any decision, but does not directly propose which projects to run.

Whatever type of instrument, it's quite clear that instruments should rather support the decisions, not make the decisions. "The thought process in decision making should be supported and not supplanted by the tools used."[104] When managers adjust the output results according to their own judging, they should get feedback on their adjustments from the instruments.[105] So they should let the tools show the new results based on the new settings; for instance a matrix charts for balance should show the future situation according to how managers currently are intending to do.

---

[100] Archer/Ghasemzadeh (1999), p. 210; De Maio/Verganti/Corso (1994), p. 184; Souder (1973), p. 907.
[101] Schmidt/Freeland (1992), p. 194.
[102] Baker (1974).
[103] Archer/Ghasemzadeh (1999), p. 207; Cooper/Edgett/Kleinschmidt (1997b), p. 47 and 49.
[104] Archer/Ghasemzadeh (1999), p. 207.
[105] Archer/Ghasemzadeh (1999), p. 211.

Already in 1974, Baker notices a trend away from models that basically are supposed to make decisions to ones that merely provide information for decisions. He gives three reasons. First, he suggests that the existing models do not take all relevant aspects of the R&D environment into account. Second, many criteria and also subjective preferences are hard to quantify. And third, as R&D has many uncertainties, managers mistrust the input data, the complex models, and consequently the resulting decision recommendations.[106]

2.4.8 Usability for portfolio goals

Figure 2.8 gives a list of the basic instruments introduced above and assigns which instruments support the quest for which of the portfolio goals of Chapter 2.3.

Goal Instrument	Strategy	Portfolio value	Portfolio balance	Sufficient portfolio output
Financial values		yes		yes, for financial output
Scoring	yes, by taking strategy criteria	yes, by taking value criteria		partly, by taking output goals as criteria
Diagrams for categorisation	yes, by categorising into project types and areas according to where strategy wants to focus on	yes, by measuring financial values on a axis	yes	
Strategic buckets	yes		yes	
Feature targets	yes, with strategic product features		partly, by ensuring that all features have projects assigned	yes

Figure 2.8 Instruments and their usability for aiming at portfolio goals[107]

---

[106] Baker (1974), p. 169.
[107] Modified and completed from Cooper/Edgett/Kleinschmidt (2000), p. 27.

Financial instruments calculate the portfolio's value and output, thus support the efficiency of the portfolio. They say whether the projects are good enough. Contrary, especially diagrams and strategic buckets foster the strategic alignment and the portfolio balance, thus support the effectiveness of the portfolio. They say whether the projects are the right ones. Both perspectives are important for a good portfolio.[108]

2.5 Portfolio review and project selection process

2.5.1 Purpose and modality

The portfolio review is the heart of portfolio management. Happening periodically, it can be combined with the strategic planning process or stand alone, especially as strategic planning is typically done once a year and the portfolio review two to four times a year. The review can last several days.[109]

At the portfolio review, the portfolio is reviewed whether it runs as planned. Moreover, decisions are made about both the ongoing and possibly new projects whether to proceed or to cancel them, or to re-prioritise and re-allocate resources. Cooper states the key issues and questions as follows.[110]

- Are all projects strategically aligned?
- Is there the right balance and mix of projects?
- Are the priorities among projects right?
- Are there current projects that should be accelerated or cancelled?
- Selection of new projects
- Are there enough resources for all these projects?
- Will executing these projects make the company achieving its business goals?

For evaluating the projects, basically every instrument or model of Chapter 2.4 can be employed.

---
[108] Based on Cooper/Edgett/Kleinschmidt (1997a), p. 23.
[109] Cooper (2005), p. 157.
[110] Cooper (2005), p. 137 and 157.

45

The whole review can be separated into the sequence of the preparation, the actual discussion and preliminary decisions, and final adjustments, described in the following sections.

Platje/Seidel/Wadman reveal that two factors determine the adequate portfolio review frequency: First, more frequent priority changes by the management need more frequent reviews and planning cycles. And second, the more all projects go according to plan, the less often re-planning is needed for re-scheduling and re-assigning resources. They further stress the need to synchronise the planning cycle of the portfolio and the planning cycles within the individual projects.[111]

2.5.2 Preparations

Before starting the actual discussion and selection of individual projects, a few things should be in place.

A strategy should be defined, either at an specific strategy-planning happening or initially at the portfolio review. It should consider external factors such as the market as well as internal ones such as the company's strengths, weaknesses, and core competences. The result is a strategic direction and focus and accordingly a rough resource and R&D budget level.[112]

All projects should have common measures and criteria in order to allow a proper comparison, common for each bucket when using strategic buckets. Before the review, each project should be evaluated separately. For ongoing projects, the analysis of their previous milestone reviews can be used, yet some companies prefer to update all project data. Furthermore, projects that do not fit some essential criteria should be abandoned before the whole portfolio consideration in order to prevent having more projects on the table than necessary.[113]

---

[111] Platje/Seidel/Wadman (1994), p. 103.
[112] Archer/Ghasemzadeh (1999), p. 208; Englund/Graham (1999), p. 54.
[113] Archer/Ghasemzadeh (1999), p. 209; Cooper (2005), p. 158; Englund/Graham (1999), p. 56.

Two groups of projects typically are still reviewed but excluded from discussion: projects in a very early stage and must-do projects. Projects in a very early stage still need to proceed. There is not enough information yet about the projects for evaluating and ranking them. And must-do projects must be done in any case. Such projects can be the ones that are well along in their development cycle and are still good and meet all criteria. Cancelling them because of new, better looking ideas – new ideas often look better – might lead to the extreme that no project ever is completed. Or must-do project can just be essential for strategy. So these projects together with their required resources are protected.[114]

Englund/Graham suggest to roughly estimate the resource need of the project ideas as well as the available resources in the organisation.[115]

Hall/Nauda recommend that, after the business directions are set by top management, middle management and technicians should generate ideas throughout the organisation and make project proposals. Then middle management gathers and prepares them, afterwards becoming again a top management decision.[116]

2.5.3 Discussion and preliminary project decisions

All projects should be reviewed together, projects far along in their lifecycle as well as new project proposals, since there might be interdependencies and all of them are within the same resource constraints. This allows comprehensive considerations of project completion or cancellation, new project proposals, changes in strategy or environment, and changes of the resources.[117]

Englund/Graham suggest conducting a number of rounds for measuring the projects against the criteria. It should start with quicker checks and get deeper once only few ideas are left. They start with the fit for the

---
[114] Cooper (2005), p. 157; Englund/Graham (1999), p. 52.
[115] Englund/Graham (1999), p. 58.
[116] Hall/Nauda (1990), p. 130.
[117] Archer/Ghasemzadeh (1999), p. 209; Cooper (2005), p. 137.

goals, then whether a sufficient market, competences and partners are available. Then technology fit, possible breakthroughs and needed marketing are overseen.[118]

Archer/Ghasemzadeh and Cooper suggest comparing the projects for determining their relative value. This can be done by pair-wise comparison or, easier especially for many projects, by scoring.[119] In case of using strategic buckets the projects are ranked in each bucket separately.[120] Englund/Graham suggest prioritising the projects mainly on their merits as they are more important than their costs. Yet the merits can still be measured against costs to determine the value for the money.[121] After this project comparison, Archer/Ghasemzadeh suggest a second step to consider the project interactions, resource limitations and other constraints.[122]

Not only the projects with the highest individual values should be considered, because some combinations of projects may produce a higher total benefit than individual projects with individual higher benefits. Apart from optimisation models[123], this appears as a thinking and discussion process.

Cooper suggests that, before killing any project, the project team should do a short presentation about their project. The rule "No project should ever be killed without the project team in the room." keeps the process transparent.[124]

Eventually, a good preliminary portfolio should be achieved.

2.5.4 Final adjustments and decisions

Once the portfolio is decided, a final review and adjustment round should be done, as suggested by Archer/Ghasemzadeh and Cooper. It

---

[118] Englund/Graham (1999), p. 58.
[119] Archer/Ghasemzadeh (1999), p. 212 and Cooper (2005), p. 158.
[120] Cooper (2005), p. 159.
[121] Englund/Graham (1999), p. 59.
[122] Archer/Ghasemzadeh (1999), p. 212.
[123] Archer/Ghasemzadeh (1999), p. 212.
[124] Cooper (2005), p. 158.

provides an overall view where the important portfolio characteristics are presented. And after having found the high-value projects in the previous step, the important objectives now are portfolio balance and strategic alignment. The portfolio should be refined by replacing some projects until these two objectives are fulfilled.[125]

Good support is given by some matrix diagrams, pie charts and prioritisation lists, showing the portfolio from different perspectives. Yet only a limited number of tools are recommendable for avoiding confusion. The effect of any adjustments should be shown again by the tools. [126]

The result now is the final portfolio decision.

2.6 Project gate process and handling of individual projects

2.6.1 Purpose and modality

Individual projects are conducted according to a process with several stages, ranging from the idea to the eventual launch. In between these stages there are reviews considering the work done so far and decisions how to proceed further, being called gates or milestones.[127] Though such a process is broadly used, as Chapter 3.4 reports from practice, in the literature Cooper/Edgett/Kleinschmidt seem to be almost the only ones who drive and elaborate on it.[128] Regarding the handling of one project in a portfolio, most research by different authors is done on the topic of different project types and how to best treat them, being described in Chapter 2.6.4.

Contrary to the portfolio review, at a gate basically only one single project is treated. And this evaluation should be deeper, based on current, adequate data. The project is given the go-decision or it is cancelled; and

---
[125] Archer/Ghasemzadeh (1999), p. 211; Cooper (2005), p. 159.
[126] Archer/Ghasemzadeh (1999), p. 211; Cooper (2005), p. 159.
[127] Cooper (2005), p. 200.
[128] Cooper/Edgett/Kleinschmidt (2000); Cooper/Edgett/Kleinschmidt (2002a); Cooper/Edgett/Kleinschmidt (2002b); Cooper (2005).

resources are allocated. And again instruments might be used for doing so. However, the gate process also is an important part of portfolio management. Therefore, the single projects should not only be viewed isolated, but with consideration of the whole portfolio too.[129]

The people deciding on further proceeding at the gates, the gatekeepers, should be competent too to provide resources and funding for the next decided project stage. Alternative funding ways that could conflict with the actual gate decisions undermine the impact of the gate process.[130]

2.6.2 Typical process

A whole typical project lifecycle with gates is shown in Figure 2.9. Which elements are especially relevant for portfolio management? Since the decisions are done at the gates – while the matter for the decisions is prepared in the stages of course –, the gates are a significant part of portfolio management. Especially relevant are the early gates 1 to 3. Here are the new projects, being decided about whether to proceed in the portfolio. Especially there the projects are not considered separately, but the screening results of several options are considered together, eventually selecting the best one or ones. Following, the stages and gates are described.

> **Discovery.** This is the creative procedure of seeking new ideas, including directed fundamental research or working with lead users.[131]
>
> **Gate 1, idea screening.** This is the first screening. In case of a go-decision, the first resources are assigned, the project is born, but still only with a tentative commitment.[132]
>
> Checklists for must-meet criteria and scoring tools for the should-meet criteria are used for focusing discussion and a first ranking. Financial data is typically not used here, since hardly available.[133]

---

[129] Cooper (2005), p. 228.
[130] Davidson/Clamen/Karol (1999), p. 16.
[131] Cooper (2005), p. 216.
[132] Cooper (2005), p. 218.
[133] Cooper (2005), p. 218.

Stage 1, scoping. The objective is to make a technical and a market assessment of the project. These assessments are only preliminary and are done in a quite short time. Work is done on the desk and by asking people as salespersons, key users as well as people from development and production, but with little or without technical research. [134]

Gate 2, second screening. Basically, gate 2 is a repeat of gate 1, but it is more rigorous now and uses the information obtained in stage 1. Must-meet and should-meet criteria are used, extended with new criteria dealing with customer reactions and legal and technical aspects. If the project obtains again a go-decision, it will move to stage 2 where resource spending is heavier. Again checklists and scoring tools are applied, and additionally a rough calculation of financial return. [135]

Stage 2, building the business case. The result of this stage is a complete business case for the project: an agreed product definition, a detailed project plan and a justification that the project is valuable for the company. Detailed investigation is done here on all aspects as customer research and technical appraisals. [137]

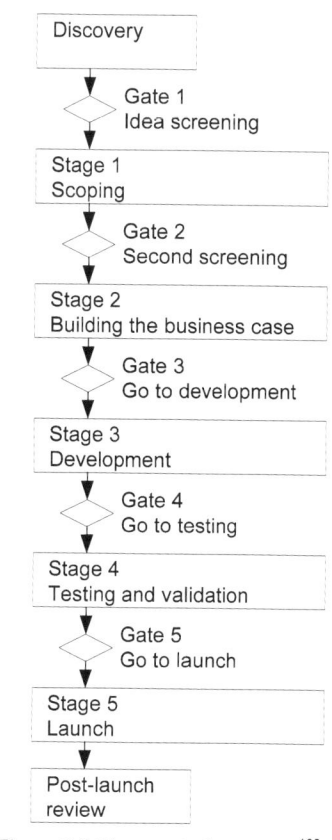

Figure 2.9 Stage-gate framework[136]

---

[134] Cooper (2005), p. 218.
[135] Cooper (2005), p. 219.
[136] Cooper (2005), p. 211.
[137] Cooper (2005), p. 220.

Market research is done to find out the customer's problems, needs, preferences, and which product they need. If the initial idea was just to introduce a new product in a completely new market, it might even be unclear which product to develop when entering this stage; but here it finally has to be decided. The customers can be asked about their work and their needs; and they can be shown a proposed product in order to estimate their reaction and acceptance.[138]

Technical feasibility must be evaluated. In contrast to stage 1, here preliminary design and laboratory work might be done, but should not grow to a full development project. Feasibility and costs of manufacturing as well as supply sources are evaluated.[139]

Furthermore, detailed legal, patent and regulatory assessment is done. Finally, a detailed financial analysis is calculated.[140]

Gate 3, go to development. Being the last gate before the development stage, here is the last decision where a project can be refused before committing much spending and resources to it. After passing this gate, all project plans are approved, and the complete project team is designated.[141]

First, the detailed activities of stage 2 are reviewed in terms of if the activities were done, if they were done in good quality and finally if their result is positive. Second, the project is checked again according to must-meet and should-meet criteria, similar to gate 2, but with more detailed information. And third, financial analyses are considered, due to the following heavy resource spending.[142]

Calantone/Di Benedetto/Schmidt regard screening and deciding at this point as one of the most critical activities, since here new ideas are scrutinised, pursued further with additional resources when

---

[138] Cooper (2005), p. 220.
[139] Cooper (2005), p. 220.
[140] Cooper (2005), p. 220.
[141] Cooper (2005), p. 222.
[142] Cooper (2005), p. 222.

promising, and set on-hold or cancelled otherwise.[143] A go-decision means much more resource spending and, in fact, makes a bet that this project and product will succeed in the market.[144] They cite several studies providing evidence of the strong relation of proper initial project screening and product performance.[145]

Stage 3, development. The main task is technical development work. Besides, activities of other aspects are done, such as obtaining customer-feedback and making test plans, market launch plans, and production plans.[146]

Gate 4, go to testing. The developed product is checked in terms of quality and compliance with the original specifications. Further, the product and the project are checked whether they are still attractive.[147]

Stage 4, testing and validation. The product itself is tested, and also the production process, customer acceptance, and financial aspects. If the results are negative, the project goes back to stage 3.[148]

Gate 5, go to launch. This is the final gate, after which market launch and full production starts. The project can still be cancelled here. Again, the activities and their results of the previous stage are reviewed; these are the testing results, the expected financial return, the products readiness for launch, and the appropriateness of launch and production plans.[149]

Stage 5, launch. Production starts and the market launch plan is implemented. Production equipment is installed. Selling begins.[150]

Post-launch review. There are usually two post-launch reviews. The first is done about 2 to 4 months after launch when the first launch results are available. The project team has its project still fresh in mind. Especially at this review, the company tries to learn from the project;

---

[143] Calantone/Di Benedetto/Schmidt (1999), p. 65.
[144] Calantone/Di Benedetto/Schmidt (1999), p. 67.
[145] Calantone/Di Benedetto/Schmidt (1999), p. 67.
[146] Cooper (2005), p. 222.
[147] Cooper (2005), p. 223.
[148] Cooper (2005), p. 223.
[149] Cooper (2005), p. 224.
[150] Cooper (2005), p. 225.

its strengths and weaknesses are assessed; and the key issues for doing it better next time are determined. The first sales and production figures already are considered, and necessary corrections are done.[151]

The second and final review is done after 12 to 18 months when the product is stable and the commercial results are well know. Only here, the project team is disbanded; the project comes to an end; and the product becomes a regular product. Latest results are used to assess the whole project and product performance: revenues, costs, profits, and timing are compared against the plans of gate 3 and gate 5.

2.6.3 Two decision steps at each gate

The gate process is a part of portfolio management. Hence, when investigating a certain project in detail and making decisions about it at the project gates, the rest of the portfolio should be considered too. This can be achieved by doing the gate decisions in two steps: The first one considers the individual project while the second one considers the portfolio.[152]

The first step, looking only at a certain project, takes some absolute criteria each project must meet. Instruments as checklists and scoring can be applied, comparing their outcomes against a predefined minimum level. The decision result is to go on or to abandon the project.

The second step looks at the whole portfolio. It makes a prioritisation of this individual project within the portfolio, considering all active and on-hold projects. Further, the impact of the project is evaluated, whether it improves the portfolio. Again some scoring results can be applied for the prioritisation. Practically, an existing prioritisation list of the last portfolio review can be taken to see where to position the new project. However, the decision is only about where to place the current project, without in-depth discussing or re-prioritising the other ones. Creating a decision out of this prioritisation results in a go or a hold for the project.

---

[151] Cooper (2005), p. 225.
[152] Cooper (2000), p. 29; Cooper (2005), p. 229.

2.6.4 Adjustments for various project types

Quite a few authors attempt to categorise different project types and consequently to suggest different management methods for them.[153] And it seems generally agreed that different types of projects should be treated differently.[154]

Cooper recommends that gates can be reduced or some can be combined for simpler projects.[155]

On the other side, for projects that start with developing a new technology, Cooper recommends to establish three extra stages for this. The first one is to define the scope of the project. It is relatively inexpensive, mostly literature research. The second stage is the technical investigation. That should demonstrate the technical feasibility, thus prove that this idea is indeed worth to work on. And the third stage is the detailed investigation. Here the experiments are done and the technology is developed. Further some commercial options and products using this technology should be identified. This stage results in a technology that can be brought into some specific product development. The gate process of Figure 2.9 may now be entered at one of the first three gates.[156]

Rice/O'Connor/Peters/Morone too suggest proceeding highly uncertain research in an additional phase before the actual stage-gate process. There, exploring, experimenting, learning, and thus basically reducing uncertainty is done, rather than developing towards any target. Uncertainty needs to be reduced sufficiently until the project can enter a conventional stage-gate process, or it gets clear that it should be abandoned.[157] Similarly, Loch states that unknown markets or new technologies require experimentation and risk management. "An individual project cannot be managed toward milestones and product feature deliverables, but must be

---

[153] Dewar/Dutton (1986); Ettlie/Bridges/O'Keefe (1984); Dvir/Lipovetsky/Shenhar/Tishler (1998); Payne/Turner (1999); Shenhar (1993); Shenhar/Dvir (1995); Shenhar (2001).
[154] Cooper (2005), p. 229; Loch (2000), p. 253; Matheson/Matheson/Menke (1994), p. 23; Payne/Turner (1999); Shenhar (2001).
[155] Cooper (2005), p. 230.
[156] Cooper (2005), p. 233.
[157] Rice/O'Connor/Peters/Morone (1998), p. 58.

managed toward uncertainty reduction."[158] And Matheson/Menke argue that it's important to find out as early as possible which project will fail and thus must be cancelled. Therefore, the most difficult challenges of the project should be worked on first – one should have cleared all hurdles which could cause a technical failure or diminish the commercial value as early as possible.[159] As another article says, "Failure is an essential part of the process. The way you say this: Please fail very quickly – so that you can try again."[160]

Shenhar develops a classification scheme along two dimensions, namely technological uncertainty and complexity. Technological uncertainty basically depends on whether implementing new or mature technology; complexity addresses the extent of hierarchies and subsystems within the total project. Then he has observed different treatments in company practices along either dimension. Let us first consider the level of technological uncertainty. For low-uncertainty projects with well-know technology, the major consideration is to accomplish the project as planned in time and within budget, acting along a fairly formal process. Contrary, projects with higher uncertainty also bear more uncertainty with regard to planning. They need more time for developing, testing and redesigning. Two or three design cycles, this is the iteration of designing and testing, are needed. And freezing the design, this is to make further changes only if necessary, is scheduled fairly late in the second our third quarter of project duration. Therefore management needs to be much more flexible, and trade-offs are required between functions, time and money. For the complexity dimension, for low-complexity projects, he has observed rather simple control systems of mainly milestone and budget monitoring, and informal decision-making within the team. Highly complex projects have a more formal process. There is an umbrella organisation which is more concerned with coordination, directives, and financial topics than with technical ones.[161]

---

[158] Loch (2000), p. 254.
[159] Matheson/Menke (1994), p. 41.
[160] The Economist (2007), p. 71.
[161] Shenhar (2001).

Based on this uncertainty dimension that usually goes along with the time horizon, Shenhar/Dvir/Levy/Maltz further determine which project goals should be emphasised for different project types, see Chapter 2.4.6.

Ettlie/Bridges/O'Keefe investigate the differences of incremental and radical innovations. They create a framework considering a couple of factors as the technology policy and the organisation's size. The major finding is that incremental innovation is best supported by traditional strategies and structures, while radical innovation demands unique strategies and structures. Further, radical innovation is promoted by a concentration of technical specialists.[162] Short time later, Dewar/Dutton conducted a similar study, yet in another industry branch. Since they receive similar results, they assume to have found a generally valid framework.[163]

Payne states that projects differ along the three factors of project size, required skills, and urgency.[164]

However, as Payne/Turner argue, a consistent management and organisation for all projects within a portfolio is still important. A similar approach is necessary for comparing the projects, for determining the resource requirements across the projects, and for moving people between projects.[165] So how to adjust the process to each project type, yet maintain a common standard? Payne/Turner suggest that the projects should be handled in three levels, in the following stated from the topmost to the lowest one.[166]

- Integrative level. The project definition and specification needs to be common to all projects in order to ensure a common basis for comparison and prioritisation. Yet large projects may enter more details than smaller ones.
- Strategic level. In some projects, the goals for the products might be well known, but not the methods how to get there, for instance when

---
[162] Ettlie/Bridges/O'Keefe (1984).
[163] Dewar/Dutton (1986).
[164] Payne (1995), p. 167.
[165] Payne/Turner (1999), p. 55.
[166] Payne/Turner (1999), p. 57.

using new technology. For some other projects, the steps and methods of what to do are still better known than the real goals to achieve, for instance in research. Then the stepwise achievement of the product goals respectively of the steps of the methods can be assigned to the gates. Still a consistent approach for resource allocation and process tracking is provided.
- Tactical level. Planning within the project is finally free for adaptation. Large projects may have a few further levels of planning.

2.7 Combining the portfolio review and the project gates

We have portfolio reviews and project gates. And at both happenings, go/kill-decisions and prioritisation are done. So how to combine both?

There does not seem to be any recommendation on which meeting to put emphasis for decision-making or whether to treat them equally. As Cooper finds, in some businesses, if gate-decisions are proper, not many decisions and no key corrections are needed at the portfolio reviews. Other businesses make the majority of decisions at their portfolio reviews.[167] However, if emphasising heavily one of the two meetings, the following two extreme positions arise.
- Major decisions at project gates. Most decisions are done at the gate meetings, including must-meet and should-meet project criteria, go/kill-decisions, prioritisation and resource allocation. The portfolio review is considered as a check whether gate decisions work properly, focused on strategic alignment, project priorities, and portfolio balance. It might only be done twice a year. Advantages are that projects are assessed deeply at a gate meeting, that the meetings are just at the right time in the project cycle, having "real-time decisions"[168], and that the project team can attend. The latter is recommendable when significant

---
[167] Cooper (2005), p. 137.
[168] Cooper (2005), p. 228.

decisions are made about their project, yet more difficult when considering many projects of many project teams at the same time. Disadvantages are that prioritisation can appear more difficult when currently assessing only one project, and that it might be hard to find free resources when only one project is on the table for discussion.[169]
- Major decisions at portfolio reviews. The portfolio review is done more often, for instance four times a year. All projects, which since the last review meeting have passed their gate 2, are especially considered. It's somehow a gate 2 meeting with project screening for them, deciding on their further proceeding with more detailed assessments. And all ongoing projects are reviewed and can still be reprioritised or killed. In contrast, the actual project gates are rather formal checks of the project in terms of time, budget, and quality executed so far. An advantage is that prioritisation and resource allocation are easier when all projects are considered concurrently. Disadvantages are that investigation per project cannot be as detailed as when considering only one single project, and that such a comprehensive portfolio review is very time-consuming.[170]

Especially when using an approach which more emphasises gate decisions, both the portfolio reviews and the project gates provide data for each other. Since the portfolio reviews prepare aggregated data about the total portfolio, the second decision step of a gate meeting, namely prioritising, may use the data of the last portfolio review. And the insights from the portfolio review, for instance needing to correct portfolio balance, can be used to adjust the gate criteria to steer future gate decisions. In turn, at a gate meeting each specific project is investigated and assessed in detail, retrieving data which can be gathered and used for the next portfolio review.[171]

---

[169] Cooper/Edgett/Kleinschmidt (2000), p. 28.
[170] Cooper/Edgett/Kleinschmidt (2000), p. 29.
[171] Cooper/Edgett/Kleinschmidt (2000), p. 30.

Both processes are applied for the same task of project decisions, but from different perspectives. This highlights the importance of doing both properly as well as, however, imposes potential for conflicts. Whatever the balance between project gates and portfolio reviews is set, both processes must work and initiate corrections if necessary. And for integrating them and avoiding conflicts, it appears important to apply the same criteria as well as involving the same people for both decision processes.[172]

2.8 Allocating resources

Decisions about project selection are also decisions about resource allocation as doing one project and abandoning another one also means to resource the former and not to resource the latter. Yet this chapter gives a few resource-specific issues.

Cooper suggests four methods on how to allocate the resources. They do not exclude each other, hence can be used in combination.[173]

- Resources to the most promising activities. The areas of the business that seem promising should get more resources than the ones that face limited prospects. For instance, when taking the popular matrix diagram of the Boston Consulting Group, categorising the business activities by the own business position and market attractiveness, the Stars being great along both dimensions should be spent more resources on than the average business.
- Resources as needed for strategy implementation. This is a top-down method. It considers the strategy, the activities to implement it, and the required resources therefore. For instance, if the strategy defines to expand with many new products in a certain area, more R&D spending is needed just there. So one could recognise then that too many or even too few projects are running in certain areas.

---
[172] Cooper/Edgett/Kleinschmidt (1997b), p. 47.
[173] Cooper (2005), p. 99.

- Benchmark with competitors. Assuming that the average resource spending of the competitors is fairly adequate, their level might be taken as orientation for adjusting the own R&D spending. Mostly this information is only available as a total number for the whole companies, nevertheless gives orientation how to adjust the total spending. Of course the companies' differences need to be considered, for instance if the own strategy focuses on being the first innovator of a branch.
- Resources as needed by the current projects. This is a bottom-up approach, starting with the currently active or waiting projects. Assuming that the decisions on which projects to proceed are proper, just sufficient resources for them should be provided. For instance, if many attractive projects are set on-hold and wait for resources, this signals that more resources should be spent in total. So here you ask whether you provide enough resources for the current projects.

Generally, these methods might reveal some of the following three insights. First, too many projects are in the pipeline, running or on-hold and waiting for resources. Second, the defined goals need to be reduced because they prove impossible with the available resources. Third, some departments are identified as the bottlenecks in the whole process and should therefore get more resources.[174]

Especially for the people resources in R&D projects, Hendriks/Voeten/Kroep find three sticking points. First, project results and the time schedules are very uncertain. Second, knowledge is essential, yet scarce; hence almost everybody provides a small piece of his specific information. And third, human ingenuity depends much on the people's true involvement and motivation.[175] Based on these findings, these authors state that how much a project is split up between different people makes a significant impact on their devotion to the project. They use a project-scatter-

---

[174] Cooper/Edgett/Kleinschmidt (2000), p. 25.
[175] Hendriks/Voeten/Kroep (1999), p. 185.

factor, calculated as the number of people involved in a project divided by the project's workload in men-years. A higher factor, thus smaller work parts split up between more people, brings more flexibility, yet reduces devotion. Hence, for devotion, efficiency, and effectiveness, the factor should be as low as possible, basically desiring a factor of 1. However, this is not possible since many different specialised skills are needed. As a solution, they suggest to introduce three different groups of project members, having different resource dedication profiles.[176]

- All-round members. They are the core team and need to have the general knowledge of the project. And they do the main part of the work. Yet problems can occur that require an expert to be solved.
- Experts. The organisation has a few experts who posses the very specific knowledge that is needed in the projects. They are not assigned to any project but are pretty free to help when needed. They act as coaches and major source of information.
- Service employees. Some tasks are the same for every project and can be done routine-like. So when they incur, the project team just asks for getting them done as a service, done by a flexible pool of service employees within the organisation or even externally.

In a study on two companies, Engwall/Jerbrant attempt to find the general, thus not organisation-specific problems in organisations with project portfolios, thus multi-project situations. They find four issues. First, the projects are much interdependent. Second, portfolio management is mainly occupied with project prioritisation and resource re-allocation. Consequently third, a tough competition for resources exists between the projects. And consequently fourth, management is occupied with short-term problem solving. These authors call this the resource allocation syndrome. Furthermore, they try to find the causes and make preliminary suggestions. On the side of resource usage, first, project scheduling might fail and, second, too many projects are ongoing in relation to the resources. On the side of

---

[176] Hendriks/Voeten/Kroep (1999), p. 187.

resource supply, first, management accounting and its incentives might be bad. Their study reveals a case where the unit is just paid for time spent on R&D, lacking incentives for increasing productivity or leaving slack reserve resources. And second, opportunistic behaviour of project managers. One manager has realised that he can achieve to get the best people assigned to his project by driving it in such a crisis that highest priority and the best people are needed to make it survive at all.[177]

2.9 Success and influence factors

Literature has put much effort into revealing which factors in portfolio management are important for succeeding with it. First in this chapter, some studies are reviewed which basically attempt a meta-review about success factor literature. I do not cite any single factors from these, since, first, they only list but don't explain them and, second, several long lists would not make sense here. But furthermore in this chapter, a representative study of Cooper/Edgett/Kleinschmidt and a study about day-to-day management by McDonough/Spital provide some factors in detail.

2.9.1 Overview of studies

To give an overview of success factor literature, this section presents a few studies which do not explore new factors themselves but survey existing literature which has done so.

Montoya-Weiss/Calantone review past studies on success factors. They also evaluate their scientific methods and quality and conclude that many lack of rigor in testing the factors' relations to success. Further, they find that the results of the studies are non-convergent, so the scopes of considered and finally suggested factors were quite various. Finally, Montoya-

---
[177] Engwall/Jerbrant (2003).

Weiss/Calantone develop four groups with in total 18 broad factors that cover every factor they have found mentioned in the literature.[178]

- Strategic factors: product advantage, technological synergy, company resources, strategy, and marketing synergy.
- Development process factors: professional technical activities, professional marketing activities, protocol, top management support and skill, professional pre-development activities, speed to market, financial and business analysis, and costs.
- Market environmental factors: market potential, market competitiveness, and environment.
- Organisational factors: internal and external relations, and organisational factors.

Dooley/Subra/Anderson do a study with the aim to gather all factors from literature and to reveal how widely these were in fact adopted in organisations. They group all found factors into eight stages of a stage-gate process and four additional categories. Their findings of adoption rates show that highest adoption is given at strategic implementation as project selection, goals, product strategy, and customer involvement. Adoption rates are relatively low at the front-end activities such as concept generation and concept selection and at human resource development.[179]

Cooper/Kleinschmidt group the success factors into the five categories process, strategy, organisation, innovation culture, and top management commitment.[180] McQuater/Peters/Dale/Spring/Rogerson/Rooney try to build on this and to enhance it. They combine Cooper/Kleinschmidt's factors into one group, named new product development, and suggest to add four more groups: business practices, stakeholders, the firm, and environment. They admit that there are many crossovers between these five groups, yet

---

[178] Montoya-Weiss/Calantone (1994).
[179] Dooley/Subra/Anderson (2002).
[180] Cooper/Kleinschmidt (1995b).

argue these broadened scope is needed to cover all issues that have direct or indirect influence on R&D.[181]

Brown/Eisenhardt find that the literature has three different streams about what R&D success is based on. First, what they call the rational plan. It is based on careful planning, a superior product in an attractive market, a competent well-coordinated cross-functional team, and top management support. Second, the communication web. Its factor is merely communication of the project teams, internally as well as externally, stimulating the R&D performance. Thus the team has the major role for success. And third, disciplined problem solving. The project teams relatively autonomously solve the problems. There are heavyweight project leaders and a strong top management with a strong product vision. Basically, the project team impacts the R&D process performance, while management and also project leaders impact the product concept effectiveness.[182] Now, Brown/Eisenhardt develop a model that combines all three directions. Their result, basically, says that, first, R&D process performance is impacted by the project teams, top management support, available resources, and information. Second, the project leaders, top management, and the customers create a product vision and impact the product concept effectiveness. Finally, both R&D process performance and product concept effectiveness together with the market make the financial performance.[183]

Kahn/Barczak/Moss develop a framework that groups best practice into the six categories strategy, portfolio management, process, market research, people, and metrics and performance evaluation. For each category, they define four levels from poor to best practice. For each level in each category, they describe the modality of company practices they assume there. Basically, best practice levels have introduced more sophisticated activities and take into account more factors than lower levels.[184]

---

[181] McQuater/Peters/Dale/Spring/Rogerson/Rooney (1998), p. 129.
[182] Brown/Eisenhardt (1995).
[183] Brown/Eisenhardt (1995), p. 346 and 366.
[184] Kahn/Barczak/Moss (2006).

Despite best practice, a company definitely should also introduce and adapt a portfolio management process that fulfils its individual needs. One study by Loch goes even so far to say that there is no valid best practice, only a best approach how to design the system in the own company. However, his study also implies that, in the company he has investigated, the best-practice process was badly executed due to insufficiently trained managers.[185]

2.9.2 Some concrete factors

Cooper/Edgett/Kleinschmidt regularly conduct some best practice studies. The results of one of their recent ones are shown here[186], yet only these ones focusing especially on portfolio management. To a few issues, some comments of other authors are added.

R&D strategy
- R&D goals are aligned with the overall business goals. And people are aware of the role of R&D in achieving these business goals.
- Strategic areas to focus R&D efforts on are defined.
- Long-term R&D goals clearly defined. Such a goal, for instance, can be a certain share of sales for the next five years that comes from new products.
- Long-term view of R&D. Not only short-term activities are done.
  The balance between long-term and short-term could also go along with ensuring continuous product launches. If for instance aiming at launching one product every quarter, the portfolio must comprise projects for launching one next quarter as well as – depending on the development time of course – all the quarters ahead.[187]
  Besides the comfort of short-term projects compared with long-term ones, another cause for missing long-term projects is a lack of strategy that would give any direction where to strive for.[188]

---
[185] Loch (2000).
[186] Cooper/Edgett/Kleinschmidt (2004a); Cooper/Edgett/Kleinschmidt (2004b); Cooper/Edgett/Kleinschmidt (2004c).
[187] Cooper (2005), p. 112.
[188] Cooper/Edgett/Kleinschmidt (2000), p. 23.

- Strategic buckets in terms of money or person time allocated to different project types or different strategic areas.
- Product roadmap. This is the view of how to reach the desired objectives. Further, it helps making sure that the capabilities are in place when needed. Beside the product roadmap, a technology roadmap may be used as well.

Albright/Kappel further argue that a roadmap links strategy with the product plan and the technology plan, enables technology plans on company-level and thus makes the technology usable for all units, focuses on long-term planning, improves communication and ownership, and focuses planning on the high-priority topics.[189]

Portfolio management

- Portfolio contains high-value projects. These are profitable, high-return projects with solid commercial prospects. Therefore, a company should use financial calculations which consider probability and risk, rank the projects along a cost-benefit index, and as well use non-financial instruments such as scoring.
- Portfolio has good balance between short-term and long-term, low-risk and high-risk, across markets and technologies and so on. Periodic portfolio reviews with, for instance, pie charts that depict these allocations give help.
- Allocation of resources and spending reflects the business strategy. So the resource split across project types, markets, business areas and so on reflects the strategic prioritisations.
- Projects are ranked and prioritised. Thus the efforts are focused, and other projects are cancelled.
- Good balance between number of projects and available resources. Thus not more projects are done than can be handled properly. Otherwise, either just too many projects get started, or R&D spending was set insufficiently.

---

[189] Albright/Kappel (2003), p. 31.

- Project portfolio that is aligned with the business goals and strategy.
- Formal and systematic portfolio management system for selecting projects and allocating resources.

For the instruments and perspectives used, Griffin states that it appears important to provide several aspects as "the best do not succeed by using just one new-product-development practice more extensively or better, but by using a number of them more effectively simultaneously."[190]

Resources
- Resources are assigned based on project merit.
- Adequate resources are assigned for R&D.
- Project teams are focused. Thus the team members do not handle too many projects at the same time.
- Members of an R&D team are focused on R&D, thus are not loaded with many extra tasks.
- Dedicated R&D group, being cross-functional and only doing R&D.

R&D process
- Emphasis on pre-development work. New ideas are fleshed out to clear product definitions and business cases; the merits and opportunities are assessed. The project plan is mapped.
- Measurement of project performance. For instance success, profitability, or net present value. Moreover, the people are mobilised by what they are measured.
- Measurement of the R&D process. This is about how efficient the projects follow the process and if the project gate reviews are done properly.
- Tough and demanding gate reviews where projects really get cancelled if necessary.

McDonough/Spital conduct a study on the success factors in day-to-day management. They define success along two measurements, achieving the

---
[190] Griffin, Abbie (1997), p. 431.

broad portfolio goals and more short-term the proportion of projects being successful in the market.[191]

Portfolio goals
- Core teams for projects. The proportion of people working only sometimes on a specific project should be kept low, especially for high-uncertainty projects where much learning is required.
- Backlog of projects should be kept short. Especially in uncertain and dynamic markets, projects in backlog prove inflexible and quickly obsolete.
- Slack unallocated resources available as reserve. In case of unexpected problems in a project, these additional resources can be reallocated without hurting another project. 10 % seem to be a reasonable proportion.

Project success
- Focusing resources. Thus not too many projects should be started. Then the active ones can reach the market more quickly and with higher quality.
- Reviewing the portfolio periodically. They found a higher frequency, for instance quarterly, better as it reduces the feedback time, thus reducing uncertainty and allowing quicker corrections. Yet the optimal frequency depends on project development duration and the industry.
- Enhance resources against time delays. When a project falls behind its schedule, it can either be allowed to just take a longer time or it can be resourced heavier, attempting to still meet the schedule. It seems that being less tolerant against slipping and thus providing additional resources gives better results. Externally, a delay causes a later market launch which is mostly a disadvantage. Internally, quicker project completion gives a more motivating feeling of causing an impact to the people.

---
[191] McDonough/Spital (2003).

2.10 Some opinions and thoughts

Some interesting opinions and thoughts on a few matters are described here. However, these statements are not sufficiently clear and unquestionable for marking them as kind of success factors.

Philosophy for killing projects and changing resource commitments

Should a good and well-running project be cancelled or downgraded in priority because just an even better and promising one has emerged? Two philosophies exist. According to the first, resource commitments are not firm. Resources can be moved from one project to another, providing the flexibility for an optimal resource allocation. According to the other one, resource commitments are quite firm. At least if a project is still a good one, resource commitments must be kept.[192]

The advantage of the first, flexible method is the flexibility of allocating resources to the best projects at every moment. The disadvantage is that starting and holding the projects and shifting resources is not seamless; it costs time and resources. Further, maybe most importantly, it is hard to maintain a team's moral and commitment to a certain project if they must fear it gets cancelled tomorrow, even though they do well. Finally, newer projects mostly shine brighter than those just struggling in the development phase. So the advantages of the fixed-resource method are the maintenance of the team's moral and avoiding costly resource shifting, but at the cost of flexibility.[193]

Prioritising the ongoing projects

Also within the ongoing projects, a prioritisation should be stated. One can argue that this is not necessary since there are only three categories of projects: ongoing, on-hold, or abandoned.

---
[192] Cooper/Edgett/Kleinschmidt (1997b), p. 48.
[193] Cooper/Edgett/Kleinschmidt (1997b), p. 48.

However, setting prioritisation and thereby different levels of importance for the running projects makes sense. Although all of them are resourced, the high-priority ones might still get more resources in order to complete them in time while less important ones may slip a little.[194]

High uncertainty causes high priority

High-priority projects are those with high importance and high uncertainty. This is because importance is related to estimates of the market, environment, and technology, of which uncertainty increases by a longer time scale. Therefore even projects with the same level of importance but a lower uncertainty should be given lower priority than the high-uncertainty ones.[195]

Central process organisation

Davidson/Clamen/Karol suggest that the portfolio management processes should be designed by a central organisation. This ensures that the process for managing the projects is an integrated part of the overall company management.[196]

Yet Cormican/O'Sullivan describe a central organisation as a mechanistic one that rather keeps past behaviour, while decentralised organisations are organic ones that are more dynamic and allow faster decisions, thereby promote learning and knowledge generation.[197]

Fast-changing market environment needs different success factors

Terwiesch/Loch/Niederkofler have analysed the impact of the market environment. They found that conventional product development performance is more important in slow-changing industries, while it counts

---

[194] Cooper/Edgett/Kleinschmidt (1997b), p. 49.
[195] De Maio/Verganti/Corso (1994), p. 188; McDonough/Spital (2003), p. 44.
[196] Davidson/Clamen/Karol (1999), p. 17.
[197] Cormican/O'Sullivan (2004), p. 823.

less in fast-changing industries. Yet it is open for further research to find new success factors that do count more in these dynamic industries.[198]

Cancellation willingness for poor projects depends on their innovativeness

Schmidt/Calantone find that, if a project has poor performance, managers are less willing to cancel it and more optimistic about its eventual success, if it is a more innovative project.[199]

They further argue that their research method is a pretty new one on this topic. Most studies are done using questionnaires or interviews in companies, thus are exposed to many influences and hardly allow determining causal relations. Their study was conducted in an experiment by letting managers decide on some hypothetical projects.[200]

---

[198] Terwiesch/Loch/Niederkofler (1998).
[199] Schmidt/Calantone (1998).
[200] Schmidt/Calantone (1998), p. 115.

3 Insights from practice

Now, the company practice from the interviews shall be investigated. Similar in structure to Chapter 2, the topics are considered in terms of how companies work, why they do so, and how these insights can be combined with the respective literature parts.

3.1 Strategy and portfolio goals

What the companies strive for indeed matches pretty well the five portfolio goals as named in literature in Chapter 2.3. No company has named any consideration that would not fit into any of these goals. But companies differ in which goals they explicitly consider and how they aim at them. Especially, not all companies explicitly state such goals, even if of course they have some criteria and goals they strive for. In the following, company goals are considered, structured into the same five goals of literature.

Ensuring strategic alignment

Almost all companies have stated strategy as a goal for their projects. Only two departments have not since they support other departments on their request within the same companies; hence strategy is considered in those other departments. So the remaining question only is how they strive for it.

One important issue is the handling of ideas. Naturally, creative ideas do not necessarily care about strategy when arising, yet can be striking for business. The match of ideas and strategy and the possible strictness of strategy alignment are discussed in Chapter 3.6.

Apart from an explicit strategy, most companies mentioned that they consider a potential customer value when deciding on new ideas and projects. In a wider interpretation, this is also part of implementing a strategy.

As one manager explained their core of strategy finding and alignment, "You need to understand […] which customer groups you would like to [address]. When you understand that, then you need to understand how does the customer group look like today, what environment do they operate in, what values do they have. And how will that change over time. Because […] it's the future customer that you do product development towards. So you need to understand that. And when you understand that, then you know what type of product you need to have in the future. And then you can see what type of product do you need, what type of product do we have today. And then you do a gap analysis. And then when you have this gap analysis, then you understand what you need to do in product development. So that is the basic for all this. Because if you only have good technical ideas or if you only have random ideas that you rank based on profitability, then you don't know what type of customer groups you will have. Then that is a happening based on profitability of the projects. And that doesn't really mean that you are hitting the right. If you have a portfolio with a lot of profitable projects, that doesn't mean that you address the most profitable customers."

One manager said "Now it takes about one year to develop a [product]. And it doesn't really matter whether it takes 11 months or 13 months. The important thing is that you have a good flow of innovation and that you know what you want to launch in the marketplace. So the focus now is switching from efficiency to effectiveness. Not knowing how to develop new products, because we know that. So the focus is now on what to develop and when to launch them. Because if we know that, then we will have a better chance of growing our business."

In two companies' businesses, a pretty tight relation and alignment with the customer is considered necessary. Hence, when deciding about the product and project portfolio, a major consideration is the match with the customer. "It's not really portfolio management, it's more customer management." as one manager put it. Here, strategy alignment means also customer alignment to a large extent.

Maximising the value of the portfolio

Only one company actually states a financial goal for its portfolio. This one defines the goals what to spend on R&D and which revenues to gain. Yet they strive pretty much for a product strategy as well. Their method is introduced in Chapter 4.1.

Some companies said to look at the project values when selecting. Not every interview actually touched on the meaning of financial numbers for project selection. But as nearly all companies calculate financial evaluations for their projects, they certainly take them into account for project selection as well. No interview revealed that financial project values would have low importance.

One company reports to consider the EBIT of the whole portfolio as well as of each product area.

Another one requires a certain minimum profit level for each project for being selected. Yet there can happen exceptions for strategic projects.

Of course, it is all about money. So is strategy. Targeting at profitable market segments or profitable customer groups is also a way of enhancing the value of the portfolio by then running projects addressing those markets and customers respectively. As a manager put it, "you can be fooled if you don't know which type of customer you are addressing by only measuring the project profitability."

However, the cause, why an explicit financial portfolio goal is so rare, presumably is given by the matter that financial estimations for projects often are unreliable, as Chapter 3.2.1 states. And without knowing what the individual projects will cost and earn, a financial portfolio target appears unreasonable too.

Seeking the right balance of projects

Six companies reported having some kind of balance as a portfolio goal.

A matrix diagram is a major part of portfolio management at one company. It measures future EBIT potential and the risk level of each project on the axes. Their goal is to keep balance all across this diagram. So they actively strive for high-potential projects with high risk too. Yet they admit that it is hard to find low-risk projects with high potential return. To a certain extent, they attempt to base their decisions on these balance facts shown in the diagram. Nevertheless, they know that the diagram does not tell everything; thus they have some projects too which should be questioned when only looking at the matrix. Yet they are strategically important, for instance areas with low profitability right now, but being a platform for growth in the future. Moreover, they also map the splits between different project types of various dimensions and try to keep balance here as well. Finally, they also want to have a certain part of the portfolio with a very long-term perspective. But this comes into conflict when resources are scarce because then there is always a tendency to favour projects with quicker earnings.

One company has set the balance between short-term and long-term projects as an explicit portfolio goal. Basically they go for it by applying strategic buckets. There they have three areas with different time horizons which are assigned a quite constant split of spending. Their approach is explained in more detail in Chapter 4.2.

Another kind of balance was reported by two other companies. Within each product area, they have quite few, but large projects. These projects are in different stages of their lifecycle. So they try to balance each portfolio for having a cash cow as well as an investment case at any point in time. Basically, this is done with different generations of the same product line. Let us assume three such projects in the portfolio for instance. First, they have the old generation as cash cow. This product sells already on the market, delivers revenue and needs only very little maintenance. Second, they have a new product which is just about to finish development. It gets launched and starts to sell, becoming the cash cow in the next phase. And third, there are projects preparing the next generation. They are still at the beginning with maybe even much research.

Apart from portfolio balance, three companies mentioned even the organisation of the company or group as an important part of ensuring balance. Having business departments and a specific research department already supports the split between short-term and long-term projects. And balance between product areas can be achieved basically by already grouping the company into departments accordingly. Chapter 3.7 investigates the topic of portfolio management by organisation in more detail.

Ensuring a sufficient portfolio output for reaching the product innovation goals

About half of the companies have a target that the portfolio should achieve. Yet these targets are of pretty various kinds.

As described more detailed in Chapter 3.2.5, three companies set targets for certain product features. Then they create a roadmap of individual projects for each feature of how to come there. For sure this is a quite sophisticated way of ensuring sufficient portfolio output.

Two companies set classical output targets. One sets the desired number of launches per year, being then translated back to how many projects are needed at each milestone stage for the time being, assuming that some will fail. Experience is taken into account when reckoning how long the projects will take in each stage and how many will in fact pass it and not be cancelled. The second company defines a desired share of revenue which should come from new products and attempts to create a portfolio supporting this.

Also another company reported to have used this goal of a certain sales share from new products. Though, they do not much regard this number any more and not necessarily consider it a healthy representation of their business. Their product lifetime at the customer's site is pretty long, thus the reliability requirements are uniquely high. "It is difficult to say that good

R&D is new R&D." They believe that a good design changes smoothly step by step in technology, but not with a completely new design.

As already mentioned above for financial goals and described in Chapter 4.1, one company sets desired levels for future revenue and R&D spending. Then the task is to initiate the right projects which should receive this R&D spending and yield this future revenue. This is kind of an output goal too.

Matching the number of projects with the available resources

Some companies reported that they try to match the number of projects and resources in a better way. Though all of them are somewhat aware of this matter, no company states this as a real portfolio goal. Indeed, starting not more projects than can be resources seems to be an important side condition rather than a goal for a portfolio where to go.

Conclusion

The interviews hardly revealed any reasons for choosing certain goals, especially as not all goals in practice are as explicitly defined as in literature.

All companies, which are not directly requested by other internal customer units, strive for a kind of strategy or customer value. As Chapter 3.6 shows, in highly uncertain research businesses, the customer value counts for project selection rather than a strict product strategy.

Rare are dominant financial portfolios goals, presumably because of the unreliable financial numbers for individual projects

Half of the companies attempt explicitly to maintain a balance in terms of time horizon or risk.

Even tough in some case not clearly distinguishable from strategy and finance, the goal to ensure portfolio output, only recently added by Cooper as stated in Chapter 2.3, indeed makes sense. Relatively many companies aim at this goal, yet in very different ways.

The goals depend on each other as strategically selecting profitable costumer groups increases portfolio profitability, and sufficient portfolio output might just aim at fulfilling strategy.

Apart from certain goals, one manager concluded that a company needs three forces to perform well. First, the marketing people with their knowledge what the customers really desire to get. Second, the engineers with their enthusiasm and their ideas. And finally, the bean counter as the company eventually needs to pay it all.

3.2 Tools for project evaluation

First, this chapter introduces the observations from company practice for the individual instruments. Then, the last section gives a general overview of instruments use.

3.2.1 Financial value

Nearly all companies calculate some type of financial evaluations for each individual project. So they consider the expected revenues and the estimated R&D costs.

As one company reported for some larger projects and products respectively, there is not only the consideration of adding the development project at all, but also which features should be included. This can also be done be financial calculation for each feature. But this kind of market estimations appears even trickier than for a total project. Especially, the customer will consider only the total product price, not each feature's worth. Therefore they use softer measures. They try to evaluate the features more out of feeling, thinking about whether it appears to be good for business. They try to understand the feature's impact on the customer's business, financial as well as non-financial, and thereby ascribing some kind of price and financial value for the own company.

Their financial calculations are basically all about risk, as another company reported. For new project proposals, they assume fairly similar revenues for each project because, when the launch is such a long time away in the future, they don't know which product will be more successful than another one. Thus the project value is basically determined only by the estimated development costs and the risk of failing. If they were to assume different future revenues, they would end up with completely different project values, although based on highly unreliable market predictions; such commercial evaluations are done only later when being closer to the launch. The risk is considered by setting the risk level for a project at the average risk level or, as assessed, at a lower or higher level. They also consider that a project being close to a certain milestone bears less risk for reaching it than one that is still far away. The same procedure applies to development costs: there are average development costs from experience, each project can be set equal to them or be adjusted to higher or lower ones. However, they too report a significant disadvantage of this kind of risk consideration as "you get punished for knowing about the risk". If they don't know anything, the project's risk is estimated as average; and if some risk is uncovered, the project loses value by increasing the risk level. Still one benefit of financial tools is that they increase the awareness for financial aspects, especially the loss of value when delaying a project.

Similarly another company uses rough estimates of development costs and revenues. Their products are not too complicated from a technical point. Therefore they just know from experience what a project of this kind will cost and what it will earn. Moreover, they have a large number of projects, somewhat compensating each others deviations from the estimates, resulting in a pretty predictable overall result.

In one company, only larger projects get a financial value calculation. Notably, they also calculate it at the last milestone before market release and then again when the product has been in the market for a while. They compare what they beforehand expected the project to gain to what it does in reality. In case of significant deviations, they can ponder on what was wrong with their estimates, which assumptions failed and thus learn for the next project. This kind of recalibrating the system does not make it perfect since many new variables come along with each new project. Nevertheless it makes it better. This procedure does as stated in literature in Chapter 2.6.2, where an additional project review a while after launch is recommended too.

One company reported that in the past they were trying to translate everything into financial numbers and to maximise profit, but they abandoned this approach because it didn't work well. Major problem was the comparison of so different projects in so different stages. Early projects only allow rough estimations; more advanced ones deliver facts more precisely. Those different stages and approximations were difficult to be taken into account. Now they try to avoid too much mathematics at all due to the uncertainties.

One company has found three financial parameters for a new project: project cost, feature improvement, and the product cost. The improvement of a product feature should provide an increase in the selling price. And when improving a product, they also try to improve costs such as production costs. And for these two benefits, the project costs are spent. Hence these three parameters of a business case are the basis for the profitability of a project, which is among the major criteria in this company.

Conclusion

Though money might be a major factor in a company, the uncertainty in forecasting it is a major problem. So no company can completely avoid financial calculations, they are for sure standard instruments and supports. Nevertheless, financial instruments are still not considered as the best and only ones. This is fairly in line with literature recommendations. Uncertainties and – even worse – different degrees of uncertainties within each project make especially comparisons between projects fairly difficult.

Therefore, a practical solution is taking rough estimations from experience, as individual estimations might fail anyway.

3.2.2 Scoring, checklists, and rankings

Merely a few companies reported to have a formal prioritisation system through the portfolio. One of them only has priorities as high, average and on-hold; the others have a ranking list. One applies a ranking list only for less important product improvement and cost reduction projects, somewhat in the function of a queuing list.

One company reported that they have used scoring systems. But now they try to evaluate the impact of their products to the customer, which is more sophisticated than scoring. Scoring has quite soft questions as strategic fit and so on. Analysing the impact is more strictly. They start with technical characteristics and try to estimate the financial impact for the customer. Their prioritisation list is created by that way and used at portfolio reviews. Indeed it is used as support which projects to resource first. There even small project can get ahead of bigger ones if they are more important.

Having a fairly sophisticated portfolio management system, one company argued that they actually don't need a ranking since their strong pursuit for strategy determines the projects. For doing that, they use the feature targets instrument introduced in Chapter 3.2.5. Strategy determines features or product attributes that should be achieved by the projects, having a few projects to strive for each feature. That instrument somewhat transfers the priority decision to the higher level of prioritising the features, but reduces direct priority competition of individual projects. Indeed, all companies that use these feature targets do not use a formal project ranking.

Only two companies use a classical prioritisation list created from scoring a set of criteria. One reported to have criteria as if the technology already is part of the portfolio, if new features are added by this project, if it is for setting up a new market, if the market is ready, if the own company is ready, if the technology is mature, if the market is existing or newly created by this undertaking. Both evaluate the criteria subjectively by persons rather than by calculations, adequately for those soft criteria. Yet the company argued that many people give the different inputs, thereby reducing the bias of any single person. These people come from marketing, product management, and technology. Both companies clearly state that these scoring results are only for support and do not at all make a decision. The prioritisation always is adapted according to people's final considerations. For instance, an important high-potential project could receive a bad score because of high risk. One would cancel it when just considering the score. "So if you don't know the background you may take completely wrong decisions." Moreover, project scores which are close together are simply considered the same and need further discussion to prioritise in case of resource conflicts.

One of the companies mentioned above established a special way of how to create the scoring. At their yearly portfolio review, everybody rates along some criteria when the project leaders present their projects. Afterwards, the management goes through the projects and scorings to make decisions. However, they realised that already while listening to the project presentation they got their feeling on how to handle a certain project. Mostly, without scoring they would have come to the same result. Nevertheless it makes sense. Since people have to fill out the scoring tool, they are forced to listen and to capture the information. So they have to care also about projects of other areas. So the advantages of the tool are to give a structure, to enforce the people to actively listen to all projects, and thereby to promote the discussion and to learn from each other's projects.

Checklists for project prioritisation are used by no company. They only use it at milestones in order to check if all requirements are fulfilled.

Conclusion

Only few companies use classical scoring and prioritisation. Those which do are fully aware that the calculated result ought to incite thinking and discussing, not replace them. In the light of this view, the disadvantages named in Chapter 2.4.2, such as precise results with yet high uncertainty behind and lack of considering efficient resource allocation, do barely matter. For one company, anyway, the happening, where all included people actively have to think about all projects, counts more than the actual scoring outcome itself.

Others create a ranking, but by impact analysis rather than working through criteria since they consider such criteria as too soft, or even derive project priority just from the strategy because it's most important. Both somehow reflect the fact that companies indeed prefer a direct way of decision making, feeling uncomfortable with anything that puts calculations in between the input and the result.

So the advantage given in literature, that scoring provides rigorous numerical results while demanding only soft input, can be seen as disadvantage too. And though strategy could be taken as a criterion, direct strategic link and thereby prioritisation can be preferred.

The variety as presented in literature in Chapter 2.4.6, offering different important criteria for different project types and different project stages, is not at all used in practice, let alone all the models which basically are more sophisticated scoring tools.

3.2.3 Diagrams for categorisation

Any kind of diagram can be quickly created out of some project data by a computer. So do companies. Yet a systematic use of diagrams for classifying projects was only reported by one fourth of the companies.

The company with the most extensive systematic use has introduced a matrix chart for initial screening their ideas. One axis shows the fit for the company in terms of technology and production process; the other axis has the value for the customer. Then they try to pick the ideas being high on both axes and evaluate them further. Another matrix diagram there shows future EBIT potential on one axis and the risk level on the other. This is the fairly popular version already introduced in Chapter 2.4.3. But there are no bubbles because the high number of projects would make this too confuse. Thus they just split each axis into three ranges, resulting in nine areas in the chart. Then the projects are each just written into the matching area. They try to keep balance by this and to have projects in every area. Instead of EBIT, they previously tried return-on-investment on the axis. But there only small projects have appeared good; and all large projects were set to the bottom end of the axis. They have also tried other measures on the axis, but found them to complicate. It should be as simple as possible. Another matrix diagram shows existing versus new technology, and existing versus new application.

A bubble diagram in another company shows risk, mainly for the own development success, on one axis and the prioritisation from scoring points, having different criteria as different kinds of risk and strategic importance, on the other one. The bubble size reflects the business need and importance of the project. It happens that most projects end up in the middle. Yet a few stick out with fairly low risk. However, the major advantage of this graphic instrument appears to be its kind of structuring and promoting the thinking and discussing of the decision makers.

One company shows a matrix with new versus existing markets on one axis. The other axis measures new products versus existing ones. But they have experienced that either classification often remains quite unclear in practice and most projects end up in the middle. Therefore, they use it only as one aspect among others and to assist discussion. Moreover, they reported to create quite plenty of pie charts as money spent per market segment, per product in a market segment, and in domestic and export markets; R&D spending per technology; spending on improvements of current products, new versions of current products, and next generation products. However, none of them is a key element for decision, but merely used as just another aspect for supporting discussion.

One company reported to often discuss in terms of long-term and short-term, low-risk and high-risk and so on. But they do not apply a certain instrument for that.

Conclusion

The real usage of diagrams cannot be assessed here as not every quickly computer-created diagram has been mentioned in the interviews. However, diagrams are mainly taken in a loose, easy-going way to show some aspects; none of them is dominant but all somewhat assist the discussion. Only few companies take a systematic approach with diagrams and try to build their decisions on them.

Seemingly, the reasons are that each diagram only shows one small aspect, but do not deliver such clear results for regularly using it as a major part – that too touches the theoretical aspect that diagrams show only information, but do not at all suggest any decision. Further, classification in a matrix chart might be unclear, ending up with most projects in the middle anyway. One the other hand, those who use it like it for visualising balance and categories or just because of its way of structuring and promoting discussion.

Indeed, their visual support seems to be the major strength of these graphic instruments, while the weakness often is lack of a clear outcome.

3.2.4 Strategic buckets

One third of companies uses a kind of predefined shares how to allocate their R&D money.

A fairly sophisticated strategic buckets approach is deployed by one company. The whole portfolio is structured into three areas: product maintenance, applied research, and the main development portfolio. A constant split of money allocation is assigned to them. Within each of these three buckets, own portfolio management processes are established, adapted to specific needs and partly introducing strategic buckets again. More about this practice is explained in Chapter 4.2.

Another company reported that they are just about to change their allocation. Thus when starting new projects, they prioritise this area that now should grow. However, an arising interesting project will be taken in any case, regardless its area and whether it will mess up this balance.

One company defines its resource split across the business areas annually on the strategic planning meeting. They consider various factors such as how fast the businesses' technologies move, the current market position, how fast the competitors move, and the own business plan. So the spending gets adjusted for a period of time. Yet it's an ongoing process and gets continuously evaluated.

The interviewed research department of one company is split into different technology areas. The number of people working in each reflects the strategic priority of the areas, so strategic buckets in terms of people. Yet they try to improve the flexibility of shifting people between these areas depending on the demand, which is tricky yet.

One company reported that on a higher level than the interviewed unit, there is a strategy board which makes the long-term decisions on which areas to strengthen and where to take the efforts down. The units get rough frames how much money they are to spend.

A type of strategic buckets is used within the research portfolio of one company, being beside the larger development portfolio. There are two buckets. One has a certain budget to spend for trying some new interesting technologies. With the other bucket, they decide to obtain a certain new technology, possibly by developing it themselves or together with a partner or by buying it.

Conclusion

The benefit of applying different management approaches within each bucket, addressing each specific project type as new products or just improvements in the best way, was only utilised by one company. Yet some more companies use strategic buckets as a top-down approach for split across the product areas, some more flexible and short-term, some more long-term.

No company has given a certain reason why or why not to use such buckets. In general, there is tendency that rather large portfolios are split into buckets while smaller ones are not, which appears quite reasonable indeed. Moreover, the named disadvantages of Chapter 2.4.4 are introducing artificial splits without real project consideration and that not really all projects are compared against each other – yet in a large portfolio both may be rather a help than a drawback.

Further, the question seems interesting, when to prefer a split according to project type and when according to product area. The interviews do not have a direct answer; presumably it depends on how wide-spread across several business areas the company acts and how large the amount of maintenance and improvement projects is.

3.2.5 Feature targets

This is a pretty new instrument, in literature only mentioned in a much less sophisticated version as Chapter 2.4.5 says. It is used by two companies in a quite similar way; a third one has a similar approach, but for a quite specialised case.

Some features, also called factors, are defined, which the company's future products should fulfil. Each feature has its own roadmap, for when it should reach which level. These features are important ones of course; thus it is an instrument supporting strategy implementation. Then they can forecast the feature's development depending on the projects; and it becomes apparent where further projects are needed.

Figure 3.1 gives an example of one feature. At the beginning of 2007, assume this to be now, the feature stands at a certain level. When doing nothing, it keeps there of course, resulting in a horizontal line in the chart. We have the intention to improve it to a certain higher level until the beginning of 2010, named target position in the diagram. At the moment, there are two projects in the portfolio that will improve this feature, each by an estimated step of improvement. Namely, at the beginning of 2008, project A will be completed and push the feature to a higher level, given it runs as planned. Later in the middle of 2009, project B will finish and give a further impact on the feature position. Yet as the chart shows, this plan alone does not achieve our target in 2010. We need to think about further options, adding a third project for instance or enhancing one of the two existing ones.

One company reported also to forecast their competitors' feature positions, considering a competitor's current position, his past development, the possible technology, what he could spend on a certain feature, and his

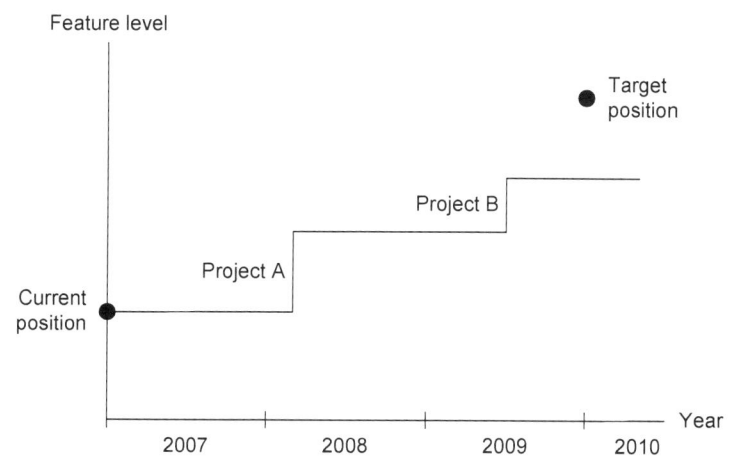

Figure 3.1 Feature target

balance across all features. Then the competitors' developments are taken into account when planning where they should aim at themselves.

The main advantage is that this instrument supports to strive for a certain strategic position. It provides a clear forecast whether and how the intended position will be achieved, "the course of a product according to the projects that are active in the portfolio". And it shows where additional projects are needed and where a project might be set to lower priority thanks to sufficient other ones. It also shows the drawback of a failing project. Before, as one company reported, they had many projects without connection, making it pretty difficult to forecast the portfolio's real impact on the future products. Now each project is linked to a certain feature and thus to strategy. One company argued that basically it's pretty reasonable to compare the portfolio's impact with the features they want to achieve.

Estimating a project's impact on a feature can be supported by looking back to past projects. For instance, when looking back on other projects of the same type and all projects ever delivered much lower impacts finally than the new one under estimation, this estimation should be questioned whether it's really realistic.

The interviews did not point to any disadvantages of this instrument, especially of course there are no insights about using it in other branches for other product types. However, constraints could arise in case of projects that are more linked together and whose impacts thus cannot just be summed up that easily. Furthermore, the split of a product's individual features and separated consideration of achieving each feature could appear tricky in some cases. Yet some approaches might be investigated how to handle such interdependencies between projects and features.

Conclusion

The development of this instrument clearly shows the ambition to keep in control of the portfolio, to know where to go, how to go there, and to do this in a straight, simple way. Yet it couldn't be more unlike the classical funnel system or mathematical optimisation systems. It is based on the principle of a roadmap; yet contrary to most high-level roadmaps, it considers individual projects.

The benefits are to have each project assigned to a strategic feature, better forecasts about future achievements, and a clearer decision support where projects are needed and where not. And by defining the priority of the features, projects priority is consequently suggested too.

A presumable limitation is that the separate consideration of individual features and the adding up of how to achieve them might be impossible or at least tricky to impose for some other product types.

In Chapter 2.3, the portfolio goal of ensuring a sufficient portfolio output for reaching the product innovation goals is named. Feature targets clearly strive for this goal.

3.2.6 Standardised playing cards

Two companies reported the use of standardised short project descriptions which in a concise form present the information needed for project comparison and decisions. One company calls them playing cards. There they only are used for the new possibilities, not for full ongoing projects, for decisions as starting, setting on-hold, or abandoning. Three pages are prepared for each possible project option. They are kind of simplified business plans after a simple assessment of few months. One slide shows the main aspects, usually four main aspects. These could be the key characteristics, the market niche and so on. Another slide shows a very early economic estimate of income and cost. As all projects are described in the same short way with the relevant data, management can quickly get an overview, compare them, and then draw conclusions and decide. This company's projects are fairly complex, having a pretty long pre-study phase. Therefore, at the next review meeting, many playing cards might be on the same opportunities again, but with more detailed information revealed in the meantime. Their playing cards have evolved over many years, originally with more technical and less market content. Now they have a better balance with more market content. Especially, their discussions tend to ending up with discussing about market aspects, while everybody already knows about technology and does not need to read about any more.

The second company uses a similar approach, called templates there, and uses them also for keeping track on the ongoing projects. They have introduced them together with introducing a common portfolio management approach over all product areas. They have a one-page overview for each project with all information, further a project overview and description, and expected financial figures. They have three areas to keep track on: quality and cost, milestone timeline, and the risk.

Conclusion

Playing cards or templates respectively are simple means for getting an overview over the projects, for decisions about project selection as well as for ongoing reviews. A common standard enables easy comparison and determines the data that really is relevant to look on. Thus it's a simple way to get the information needed for making the decisions, yet without any decision suggestions from an instrument.

3.2.7 Using tools for decisions

The previous sections have introduced and commented each instrument. Here they are considered altogether in how companies use them for eventually coming up with decisions.

Decision support

Companies never base their decisions directly on instrument results. They take instruments only for getting information and views from different perspectives at their portfolio. One manger clearly brought it to a point, "At the end of the day, I think tools only help you to an extent. Tools are not decisions-making, they help you in giving you the information of certain views to make the decision. Because by it's very nature it's [R&D] a high-risk activity. And tools can only help you lower your risk, not eliminate your risk. Or categorise your risk. They also help you to identify which areas you need to focus to reduce the risk. So tools are used as an aid to make the decision than the tool being used to make the decision itself. I don't see tools being used really make the decision. So we don't have something coming out of the tool, and when the tool says stop the project then we stop the project. No, they're giving you information depending on the urgency, the need, the potential benefit."

This statement applies to nearly all companies. The difference between the companies is to which extent they deploy tools at all. Yet if they use some, they use it as stated above. And kind of discussion leads to the decision finally.

One company pointed out that there are several aspects when looking at a project; no one is the overriding one. When being still far away from a concept, financial analysis is less. Then the analysis concentrates more, if the project is relevant to the business strategy.

One company, being pretty research-based and using barely any instruments at all, described that they have an extensive review process where experts give opinions. The final decision is taken by a council. The decision is an informal process of mainly weighting the experts' opinions. "Personal judgement is our control maker".

One might conclude two points from that. First, instruments appear unable to provide a perfect solution which companies are willing to implement directly. And second, a responsible manager takes a decision which he has thought through and considers as the best one, not just what instruments have created. That goes fairly along with the common literature opinion of Chapter 2.4.7.

Apparently, decisions often must be based on opinions and subjective arguments rather than on hard facts. This insight makes the job even more challenging, but lack of objective arguments does not even make it easier to judge one's decisions.

Discussion support and moderation

Some companies emphasised the meaning of instruments for supporting their discussion. Hence their purpose is not to present results that quickly lead to a final decision. Rather tools present the important facts and thereby even moderate and incite thinking and discussion, and not at all replace them.

As already mentioned in Chapter 3.2.2, one company has established a large annual portfolio review where scoring is used. Each project leader presents his project. There everybody needs to assess certain criteria for each presented project. Then the scoring results are used in a ranking as well as in a matrix diagram showing scoring points and risk on its axes. The fact is that everybody has to fill out the scoring tool. Therefore they are forced to listen and to capture the information, even for projects of other areas than their own. Hence the benefit of the tool is to give a structure, to enforce the people to actively listen to all projects and thereby to promote the discussion and to learn from each other's projects. Along that process everybody forms his opinion how to decide about the certain projects, even making the actual instrument outcome somewhat less important.

Two other companies have introduced playing cards, being standardised information sheets for each project, explained in Chapter 3.2.6. They do not suggest any decision. But by presenting the important facts for each project in an easily comparable form, they enable an efficient discussion.

As simple as possible

Even if only three companies have stated it explicitly, it appears that all companies try to keep their portfolio management and their usage of tools as simple as possible. The companies are fairly different in how intensively they deploy instruments and a formal process. See Chapter 3.5 for a discussion on that. Yet even companies with a pretty sophisticated system have kept it simply and straightforward to a strategic target. Calculations are very rough ones and mainly based on experience, for example for average failing rates before reaching a milestone or expected development costs for a new standard product.

One company said "We have tried to use as simple model as possible for people to be able to understand what we are trying to achieve." If people ought to take the results as support for their own decisions and then even should judge for others eventually why having decided so, the results of instruments – and their way to get there – need to be easily understandable.

Except for rough financial value estimations, calculations are barely used. "It is more like a discussion. We have tried [...] a number of years ago [...] to translate everything into economy and then have a large Excel sheet and look at what is the maximum turnover and maximum profit and minimise investment and things like that. But it does not turn out very well. Because if you have a number of [...] alternatives, some are in very early stages where you have only very rough estimates [for the next years] [...]. And others are things that might be very small and you have worked with them for a number of years and you have rather precise facts. So it is very difficult to take into account that they are in different stages of maturity and in different approximations or estimates or whatever. So it's more of a discussion."

As I have found, literature does not put as much emphasis on simplicity. Some developed tools are simple, some others rather complicate. Yet simplicity is barely mentioned as a requirement; even if it seems to be essential for an approach for having a chance of being adopted in practice.

Empty portfolio

One company argued that tools somewhat assume a starting position of an empty portfolio and a certain amount of available R&D funding, having complete freedom how to compose the new portfolio without existing conditions. In fact, the existing portfolio is already filled with ongoing projects. They have been decided earlier, do well, and certainly should be continued. Only a small share of capacity is left each year for taking up new projects. And these new projects should have synergies with the existing ones in terms of technology or market. Therefore, reality is more about expanding the ongoing tracks rather than starting something completely new.

Conclusion

No company binds its decisions to any outcome of the instruments, in accordance with the literature. In the tightest case, the outcome is taken as a guideline. For instance the ranking list according to some scoring points puts a small project with below-average profit on the bottom end; yet the managers know it is a must-do one because important for strategic purpose. Undoubtedly it is extremely important to consider not only the instrument's outcome numbers but to understand and evaluate the meaning of the projects behind. Seemingly, instruments hardly provide results which a responsible manager would be willing to implement directly without re-thinking.

Some other companies do not even expect the instruments to deliver any results. Rather they take instruments for the purpose of illustratively depicting the needed information, thereby inciting and moderating the discussion. That is an aspect I have not found in literature.

Company decisions about projects clearly focus on customer requirements. These requirements can come from direct request from external customers or internal customers within the same group. Or they can just be what the company presumes are features or functions which will be valued by the customer. And as a necessary condition in business, all this should somewhat provide financial value for the company. Instruments need to support this view as clearly and simply as possible. Companies indeed prefer a direct way of decision making, feeling uncomfortable with anything that puts inscrutable and uncertain calculations in between the input and the result. First, such complex calculations might fail anyway due to unreliable data; and second, it needs to be understandable for all the involved people who should implement it. Therefore, simplicity is an essential requirement for instruments, which wish to be adopted in practice, and therefore should get more notice in future literature.

3.3 Strategic planning, portfolio review process, and decisions there

This chapter is about regular portfolio reviews and strategy planning and, of course, about the decisions there.

3.3.1 Modality of happenings

Nearly all companies do a large strategy meeting once a year. At this happening, also the whole portfolio is reviewed. Altogether, portfolio reviews are done once a year by nearly two thirds of the companies, four times per year by one third; and one company does it twice a year. Such a portfolio review basically is also a meeting for doing all kind of decisions as selecting projects, cancelling, adjusting projects, re-prioritising, and allocating resources.

One constraint and one addition should be taken into account when comparing these numbers. As constraint, the interviewed company departments are not all at the same level in the whole company organisation, nor are their whole companies respectively groups of the same size. As addition, a few companies have additional reviews for parts of the portfolio.

Of course, as two companies have said, a review and decision meeting can also be done more often if there is a special need as a customer request for instance. Then they need to estimate if they can meet the customer's requirements as well as the consequences for the other projects.

One company, having separately a product development portfolio and a research portfolio, reviews the product development portfolio as well as the current product portfolio quarterly. The research portfolio is reviewed only twice a year; this is enough since these projects run for a long time and are not newly started that often.

In one company with pretty many projects, a few milestone reviews accrue each month, actually for individual projects only. They gather them and make a monthly milestone meeting. This company applies the feature target instrument which deploys feature roadmaps. Should a project drift from meeting its targets – this occurs pretty often as they say – they need to decide further steps as well as to adjust the related feature roadmap. These procedures altogether give somewhat a portfolio review every month. A few years ago, they neither conducted a monthly review nor had a system for measuring their features. Then, only during the yearly planning process, they worked through where the stood in each project and, pretty late, realised that they were slipping in some features. Additionally now, they conduct a quarterly review of these roadmaps.

Each product area within one company does a monthly portfolio review of its area. It's a review for keeping track on whether progress is as planned. When accruing, also milestone reviews are done there, approving that all required tasks have been completed and thus the certain milestone has been achieved. Yet no decisions are done there, these are taken more centrally.

And another company also does a small monthly review just to keep track on the status of the projects and to check whether there are any problems or conflicts.

One company has an additional monthly review for the projects on their hotlist. These are the projects that are already pretty advanced, close to launch and thus most important. Hence they review them to see which projects are still on track and which ones need to be taken off the hotlist as the will slide or fail.

3.3.2 Extent of project evaluation

Merely one company explicitly stated that they exclude existing, well-running projects from discussion. So projects that run according to plan and are far along their way, maybe even shortly before launch, are just continued without much discussion. This reflects what literature recommends, as

Chapter 2.5.2 reports. Yet they are considered in the review as existing, together with the resources they need and the markets they address. They are part of the ongoing direction of the portfolio. Therefore, discussion is done only for the – relatively little – remaining part of the portfolio where to decide about new possibilities and directions. Along with that, they try to consider the existing directions and the new possible directions somewhat separately in two tracks. The existing businesses should be considered in detail as far as data available depending on how far they have come along already. On the other side, they try to maintain an open view for new market opportunities. "If you only do detailing, you risk ending up with something you know very well. You have an exact detail plan for how to do this. But the markets are shifted; and in some year's time you will be out of the market. And if you only do this overall picture, you don't have any product development. So you have to combine this in some way. To keep a balance what we do on overall level and more in detail."

Two thirds of the companies thoroughly review each individual project at the portfolio review. Two companies do not and focus on the overall perspective. For the remaining companies, the interviews do not allow clear statements. Also the literature describes that some companies review each project at the portfolio review, and some others only review the portfolio at an overall level, aggregating the project data from the individual project milestone reviews for instance, see Chapter 2.7. One factor for how to handle this might be the number of projects. Nevertheless, most companies consider each project. Doing so provides, seemingly, more comfort for understanding the portfolio situation and for making decisions.

One company arranges their yearly portfolio review as a quite large happening. Each project is presented by the project managers. Then the projects are evaluated by a scoring instrument before decisions are made.

Another company in fact said that, at their portfolio reviews, they use the project summaries they have created at the gate meetings for each project.

3.3.3 Main purpose of the review and project selection

Nearly all companies use the portfolio review happening not only for investigating their portfolio but to result with decisions as well. So some additions or exceptions are shown here.

Two companies reported to separately hold a special meeting for starting new projects. One of them has split the portfolio into different product areas. An area manager proposes the activities he would like to do. Then a broader board, mainly consisting of business people, finally decides and prioritises. Thereby, they align the project selection according to their business focus. In this company, the real portfolio review is rather strategic and does not consider individual projects. The other company reports a similar project selection meeting. The project proposal consists of a financial calculation and a resource plan. The project is checked whether it matches with the yearly decided roadmap and the strategy. If it does not, it gets abandoned. If it fits, the business case is reviewed more in detail. Mostly, more projects enter that process; so the most profitable one will be selected. Only these projects are considered there, not the whole portfolio.

Two companies have split up their meetings. One of them has quarterly a kind of information meeting where the portfolio is reviewed, but no decisions are made. A second quarterly meeting then is the decision meeting. The other company stated that they first do a rather technical meeting where technical issues of the projects are discusses. Afterwards, there is the portfolio review that focuses more on the business side and really makes the decisions. Nevertheless, the second meeting mostly results with what was already proposed in the first one.

One company has split the portfolio into long-term projects and short-term projects. Basically, the former is product development; and the latter is product improvement. The latter projects last for less than one year. Hence, at the yearly portfolio review, they only give a budget frame for these projects, not knowing yet which ones really will be done. Contrary, the product development projects run for a few years. There, they consider which projects are currently ongoing and decide which ones to start.

One company reported that, although most project decisions are done at the yearly review, there are also some decisions throughout the year.

One company, doing its strategy planning and portfolio review together annually, stated that the task there is to sort out, to decide which options to follow and which ones to abandon. As they also said themselves, they have a classical funnel system, starting with many ideas and pre-studies which get fewer as the come more into actual product development.

Another company said that their main purpose of the yearly portfolio review is to set portfolio prioritisation and to match between the portfolio strategy and the available resources. Yet they consider each project and rank them by scoring points.

At one third of the companies, the portfolio review also provides a project prioritisation list. One company stated that they only create one on special occasions; for instance, when the need for a highly important project arises but it absolutely can't be resourced, then active projects might be prioritised and evaluated which to set on-hold or cancel. For the rest of companies, the interviews do not provide a clear statement.

3.3.4 Conclusion

The modalities of portfolio reviews are fairly mixed. Especially, a fact which I did not find mentioned in literature, apart from the classical regular portfolio review, many companies have introduced extra reviews. These are fairly adapted to each individual business case, mostly monthly smaller reviews of a certain portfolio part for keeping better track on the projects or mixtures of portfolio and gate reviews.

At the large portfolio review, most companies review each individual project thoroughly. This seems indeed to be a more comfortable way to get a real feeling for the portfolio than by only considering the big picture of aggregated data.

A prioritisation list for all ongoing projects, as recommended in Chapter 2.10, is done only by few companies.

Decisions mostly are done at the portfolio review meetings, sometimes at separate project selection meetings, and of course throughout the year when needed.

For the portfolio review, the suggested points and the sequential flow of Chapter 2.5 are strategy definition, deciding common project measurements, excluding certain projects from discussion, discussing and deciding in maybe more rounds, and making a final adjustment. In practice, strategy is first of course. Yet for the other things, the interviews have hardly revealed any certain rules or sequences. And rare are explicit project exclusions from discussion and extra adjustment rounds.

3.4 Project gate process and handling of individual projects

3.4.1 Purpose and modality

Every company runs a gate process for each individual project. This process is mostly a rather formal one, seemingly the most formal one in the portfolio management topic. One company reported that these gates impose much administrative work; yet the huge benefit is to get control of the situation and to know where they stand.

The gates basically have two functions for most companies. First, the project is assessed whether it delivers the requirements and specifications that were defined for that stage. That's the quite formal part, often kind of checking what has actually been done. And second, an outlook is done whether the project is still reasonable and needed, whether it still makes sense to bring this product in this form to the market, are the resources available, and by which priority and speed should it go on. This part seems less formal, is rather discussion-based like the portfolio review. One company separates these two functions even in terminology, at milestones looking back and at gates looking forward. So companies do pretty alike as proposed in literature in Chapter 2.6.3, considering the project deliverables as well as considering its priority in the portfolio and market prospects. It does not matter that only one company really separates it into two steps.

One company has softened the gates in their function as a transition from one project stage to the next. They try to start the next phase as soon as possible, even before the current phase is completely finished. So the stages are overlapping. They try to do as much work in parallel as possible. The benefit, of course, is to reduce the total lead time of a project. The drawback is to take additional risk since, for instance, they do already some testing before development is really completed. Since each project is somehow unique, they must decide for each project specifically when to start the next phase; it's a trade-off. "We have learned that the cost of delaying a project is much higher than the more in the risk you are taking in moving forward too early." The more likely the current stage will be completed successfully, the earlier the next one can be taken. Consequently, reaching a milestone means to have accomplished all work in the stages before. Though it does not mean to enter the next stage right now; they might already have started working on. Only milestone 2 is a strict one since there the real project start is decided and resources are allocated.

As far as the interviews have revealed, only two companies adapt their milestone process specifically to the project type. One company has different milestones processes depending on the project size, using fewer milestones for smaller ones. Furthermore, they conduct research projects which bear a large extent of uncertainty and are difficult to schedule. There they have no milestones at all, running before the actual milestone process. The other company is searching for a way to adopt such an adapted milestone process which still serves the overall performance measurements.

3.4.2 Considering the whole portfolio

This aspect is already touched by the second step named above. As the gate process, especially the gates as decision points, is an important part of portfolio management, the question arises whether only the respective project is considered at such a gate or even the whole portfolio.

One company answered "That's a good question. In general, we only look at the individual project. But of course you need to be aware of the other portfolio around it as well." They consider a milestone to be an assessment of the project's quality. Yet later milestone reviews are done at a higher management level in that company. And there they have still more overview about the company situation and its portfolio. And since they cannot run every project at full speed, they need to decide about the priority for going on with the certain project. Therefore, they indeed consider other projects' priorities and the company's current needs.

Another company reported that the absolutely consider the rest of the portfolio. In case of some other activity has arisen that really needs to be focused on, the project in question will be stopped. They also emphasise that gates are asynchronous events, occurring when the project is ready for the specific gate or when it is scheduled in the project plan. The asynchronous aspect applies even more to that company since they have projects of very different durations.

One company said that it is only one project that is reviewed. But they might in their assessment of the project come up with issues and things that are of great interest for the portfolio.

One company especially considers the relations to other projects, for instance the borders between the projects and the results the use from each other. These are specified when starting the project and then reviewed at the gates.

Six companies stated to definitely take care of the rest of the portfolio too when doing a milestone review. Merely two want to consider only the respective project.

Anyway, it seems that most companies have no need to answer this question that strictly. People who review project gates regularly know about the company and the portfolio. And if they see, for instance, that another project needs the resources far more urgent, they will not just ignore it due to any strict rule to consider exclusively one project. Therefore, the question is mainly relevant when creating the organisation and when designating the people for doing the gate reviews; it seems to be a great benefit if they indeed are aware of the whole portfolio and the company's priorities too.

3.4.3 Pre-studies and project selection

Some companies stated that they attempt to run projects in the early phases, when it's not sure if this is the right way, with small money and to select carefully before the heavy spending begins. So initially, pre-studies are done in order to reveal more information about the case. And before starting full-scale development, often at milestone 2, a rigorous meeting makes a decision whether to go on. Of course, this means also to accept wrong ideas and failures, yet they should be sorted out quite early. Hence this milestone is a large and pretty important one. That goes along with literature opinion.

Yet as one company reported, the very first beginning of a project, so when beginning to investigate a new idea with little money, is a rather diffuse process, especially since ideas can come from so many different sources.

3.4.4 Conclusion

At a gate, many companies consider both whether the work of the previous stage was properly done and the project's future prospects and relevance. Thereby many companies also consider the rest of the portfolio, mainly for setting priorities across the projects. This goes along with the suggestions of literature. Therefore, it seems to be a great benefit if the involved people at the gates know about the complete portfolio and company too.

There is an important milestone decision, often at the second milestone, where the transition from the small, cheap pre-study to the large, expensive project happens. So recommends literature.

Rarely applied is the adaptation of the milestone process to different project types, while literature has plenty of studies in this field. Yet the interviews give no information why it is not adopted in more companies.

A pretty new approach is the overlapping of stages in order to finish the project faster, while thereby taking somewhat more risk.

3.5 Various levels of sophistication in portfolio management

Apart from the question which methods they use, the interviewed companies generally populate a fairly broad spectrum of how sophisticated their methods and processes of portfolio management are. On one end, there are companies and managers who ponder about how to manage their portfolio and who have developed different processes and methods. The opposite are companies which barely use any specific methods but achieve their portfolio decisions just by thinking and discussing.

Yet judgement which one works better is tricky. First, this work does not reach as far as to evaluate the success of a company's project portfolio, thus being unable to reckon a correlation between applied methods and achieved success. Second, the interviewed companies respectively departments are in different business situations with different branches, different customer structures and different stage in the chain between the technical idea and the customer product. And third, the classification in this work what was more and less sophisticated is somewhat subjective. However, the studies citied in Chapter 2.9 conclude indeed that are more sophisticated system, thus being more formal to a certain extent and considering several aspects, brings better performance.

Building a hypothesis

Moreover, it appears interesting to explore which companies have developed a more sophisticated approach. Is there a connection between sophistication in portfolio management and the business situation? The interviews show a tendency how these may be correlated and give way to a hypothesis.

There are four companies and departments respectively which have developed a sophisticated portfolio and product management, and they are all quite close to a customer market where they basically do not know their customers yet and do not develop customised products. Their portfolio is dominated by projects that should be sold as products on a market to many essentially unknown customers. This applies to both, departments doing much research and such only doing product development. So these departments facing a typical market have developed the more sophisticated methods.

Contrary, there are five companies and departments respectively which have a less formal approach. And four of them face a strong customer relation, internally with other units within the same company group or externally with customers who demand highly-customised products. So they mostly develop each of their products customised on agreement for one or, for synergy, for a small number of customers. Here portfolio management strongly runs in alignment with the customer and is therefore less formalised. Of course these companies still need a good management of their own resources. But the decision which projects and products to strive for is rather a matter of agreement with the customers. "It's not really portfolio management, it's more customer management.", as one manager told it, meaning that what matters is to establish good bindings with good customers. And another stated "If anyone [a customer] pays for the project, then it's strategic." Especially when having internal customers, these should then take the part of have the formal project and product management.

Four companies remain that somewhat do not support this correlation. They have rather an average level of portfolio management; some face rather a market, some rather a customer binding. Neither contradict they this correlation.

Conclusion

Hypothesis: Companies and departments respectively, which directly face a market with less customer-binding and less customised products, develop a more sophisticated project and product portfolio management approach. Contrary, those, which have high binding with internal or external customers and develop customised products for them, have a less sophisticated project and product portfolio management, because their portfolio management is dominated by customer alignment.

This hypothesis could be tested in further research. More precise definitions for more and less sophisticated portfolio management approaches and for the market situation with and without customer-binding and customisation might be needed. The former could make use of the best practice framework of Kahn/Barczak/Moss, see Chapter 2.9.1.

As far as I have found, current literature generally praises more sophisticated, systematic approaches without investigating differences of the market and customer situation.

3.6 Starting with the ideas or with the markets

Theoretically, there are two extreme points: Either you start with the ideas as a classical funnel system, collect as many of the best ideas as you can find, gradually abandon the ones which have proven unattractive while still pursue the others, and finally see at which products and markets you end up. Or you start with the strategy, define exactly which customers and markets to address and thus which products you need and do not care yet about which ideas and projects actually will bring you thither.

Of course, none of the interviewed companies is as headless as the first approach suggests. They rather can be classified somewhere in the range from the middle to quite close to the strategy approach. The question arises what causes a company to stand more in the middle or to tightly align to a market strategy?

As one company explained how their ideas were handled before introducing a proper strategy alignment, "We can only do that filtering [of projects] if we know where we want to go. We can only say Yes or No to ideas like that if we know where we want to go. [...] And I've seen this. [...] The primary development people, they come to us and they say 'I have this great idea!' Nobody knows what to answer. Nobody knows whether to say Yes or No. So what is the reply from management? The reply is always 'That's a great idea, keep up to good work, develop it a little bit further so that we can see whether it makes sense or not.' And the engineers will go back, and they will develop this idea further, and they will build it, and they will refine it. And two years later, they will still work on the nuts and the bolts and make it nice and so on. And people go like 'Oh, we spent so much money on this brilliant idea, let's make a product!' And we make the product. And then once we have made the product we go like 'Shit, we have to sell it! Okay, let's make a market plan, and then we try to sell it!' And then nobody wants to buy it. Because it was the totally wrong product to sell. [...] So that's why we want to zoom in [to strategy targets] rather than just go off without knowing why we do things. What to develop is important, and when to launch it, rather than how to do it. [...] We know how to do it, but we need to know what to do."

Maybe the last sentence is an important condition for how tight a certain company can focus on strategy. If the development itself is not outstandingly difficult, if they just know how they will develop it as the cited company does, aligning every idea only to the strategy seems strongly recommendable. Yet there are companies and branches which barely can say "We know how to do it" because it's only the meaning of their research projects to find out how and whether at all they can do it.

Building a hypothesis

Of course, all interviewed companies have a strategy and do projects only if they fit. Therefore, the differentiation which ones emphasise strategy more and which ones less is somewhat unclear. Yet there are six companies which strongly and strategically define the areas to work in and which try to come up with projects there. What to do is determined by considering the market and the desired customers. Contrary, five other companies regularly come up with ideas which then are assessed whether they will provide value for the company as well as for the customers and whether they fit the company, but without strict focus of a strategic market area. They rather discover what appears possible and then assess whether it is worth being made possible. All these five companies are pretty research-based. Contrary, all the six strategy-focused companies are mainly focused on product development.

If the product development is not that difficult, one considers more the market and less the own technology. The question is what to sell; once decided it will be possible to create it. Oppositely, if doing outstanding research, it matters not only what to sell because, first, the product ready for selling is further away and, second, there is more uncertainty anyway whether one will succeed at all with the project. This observation of course is based on the fact that research bears more uncertainties than product development – that's not new. Yet, this consequent impact on companies' approaches is still interesting.

Stating the hypothesis, the stronger the projects belong to research, the more just the value of ideas is assessed rather than a strict strategy alignment.

In other words: Defining targets and knowing where to go is always a fine thing; yet the more uncertain, trickier and research-based the projects are, the less possible and reasonable precise strategy targets are.

It is always a match between strategy and ideas. At one company type, the strategy is fixed and the ideas must align. At the other one, both strategy and ideas align to each other.

Assessing the ideas' values and benefits with less market and strategy focus

So working with research and more uncertainty put more emphasis on the upcoming ideas. Of course, they need to be assessed.

One company reported that they can get ideas from many sources, and regularly more than they can do. For selection, they start with a matrix diagram for an initial screening. One axis shows the fit for the company in terms of technology and production and so on; the other one assesses the value for the customer. Of course they try to pick the ideas with high fit and high value. Interesting ideas are pursued by forming a business case with deeper analysis, estimated financial figures, risk assessment and so on. This company is explained in Chapter 4.3 in more detail.

While often driven by direct customer requests, one company said that ideas can emerge merely from a technology perspective too. Then they attempt to speak to customers, tell them what maybe is technologically possible and ask them whether they have a need for that. Then they decide whether they should proceed on those ideas with a pre-study.

One company is active in quite basic research as well as rather product development, yet high-technology products are delivered to other divisions within the same company. For the research part, if someone has a good idea, it is presented. Then they assess whether it will be an advantage and whether they should start it now or maybe in the future. For the development part, they assess deeper what the value for the future will be, what the main function and some extra functions are, and which solution can be realised by that. They try to assess whether that really will be a benefit for the customers or for themselves by making it cheaper for instance.

Another company deploys a strategy team for each large product area. Ideas basically can emerge everywhere, in these teams as well as from individuals by reading or conferences. These teams assess if an idea is interesting enough as well as look for the risks; then they decide. For such an early project, they want to find out as soon as possible whether this really is a project that can be developed. Usually many problems occur in the beginning. Then they might realise that they cannot cope with this project and should cancel it as soon as possible. So this first stage pretty works on reducing the uncertainty, as literature is cited in Chapter 2.6.4.

Addressing market and strategy

The product development companies can better state a strategy, defining by which products to address which customers. Their major uncertainty is the customer, not their own R&D. Some companies have introduced such a long-term strategy only a short time ago. Until then, they had been having their ideas, proceeding with what had seemed attractive and profitable, but not really heading for a clear direction. As the long company citation at the beginning of this chapter shows, they eventually realised that their project portfolios somewhat do not bring them towards the position where the actually want to come. Hence, they have introduced a strategy that steers their R&D projects. And also their applied research departments, where a certain outcome still is tricky to forecast, are more focused on areas and directions that are strategic. These departments rather think of how to realise the desired functions than which functions to realise at all.

Nevertheless, also a strategy-focused company eventually needs new ideas how to pursue its strategy. However, when deciding which ideas to proceed, only the ideas matching the strategy get a pass. A few companies indeed refuse as early as possible any idea, whatever so attractive, unless it supports the defined strategy. Furthermore, searching and musing about new ideas can already be focused on the certain areas directed by strategy.

The question remains what if an idea appears so striking that the company might adapt its strategy for it. So a highly innovative idea that could strive for products and markets nobody was thinking about before. Maybe there is no general recommendation for that case.

One company said that they don't start with ideas and select them and proceed with them. Yet they start with where they want to be in the future, which businesses, which countries, which segments. Then they identify the gaps between desired position and current one and try to fill it with products which would make sense for the customer in the future. "Which means that we can then start to match ideas with the opportunities." That also drives the development of concepts and products. This procedure is described in Chapter 4.1 more detailed.

One company, working with strong customer relations, aligns its product development with its customers. Merely at their research projects, they start from the ideas side; yet there it is about how to do it, not what to do. "You have ideas on how you implement [...], how to design [...] to have this certain function, but not the function itself. I think this rarely comes from below [...], it comes from the [customers] [...]."

Another company reported that, if they have a good idea with the possibility to improve features, they will start a project based on that. Yet they always check if this corresponds with the feature strategy of their products. An excellent and profitable idea for any feature will not become a project, though, unless they have decided to focus on this feature. They use the feature targets instrument, see Chapter 3.2.5. They have also a smaller part in their portfolio dedicated for more research-based activities. The focus there is based on those feature strategies, steering in which areas they want to do research. Nevertheless, steering research by the long-term feature strategy is quite newly introduced there. "Up to now it have been creative technicians that have been driving what to develop. I'm not saying that we don't still have wild ideas. But it is more steered than it has been before." This company is explained in Chapter 4.2.

Conclusion

Hypothesis: The more the projects belong to research and thus face more technical uncertainty, the more these companies and departments respectively just assess the value of ideas rather than strive for a strict strategy alignment at their project selection. Contrary, the more the projects belong to product development with less technical uncertainty, the more these companies respectively departments introduce an approach that is stronger directed towards strategy and markets.

The former group rather matches a classical funnel system, where it is important to quickly reduce uncertainty and to sort out unattractive projects as early as possible. Value assessment is done in terms of customer value and fit to the own technologies, sometimes also by asking customers. The latter group can – in ideal case – already decide at the very funnel beginning if a certain idea fits the strategy. Maybe one may call it a funnel, though with a rigorous selection at the beginning.

I have not found literature that applies such a classification scheme for the whole company approach. Yet some parts of the literature, which investigate different project types, are related to that topic and might be used for further research. Especially interesting seems the work of Shenhar/Dvir/Levy/Maltz in Chapter 2.4.6, who set different goals for projects with different uncertainty.

3.7 Company organisation, standardisation, and local and central decisions

This chapter is about running the company and thus the portfolio in different business units, especially with an R&D unit, about a standardised way of portfolio management across the company, and about at which hierarchy level to do the decisions. These are three different aspects, nevertheless influence each other.

3.7.1 Organisation of the portfolio into different business and R&D units

The interviews revealed that the organisation of the company or the group gives an important impact to portfolio management too. The matter is how to separate the different projects into different departments and thus into completely separated portfolios. Mostly the separation is somehow between short-term and long-term activities.

Splitting short-term and long-term activities

Having a specific R&D or research unit can already be used for balancing short-term and long-term projects. Such a unit rather makes the long-term projects and thereby supports the business units, which in turn are the direct interface to the market and run rather short-term projects.

Five of the interviewed companies have established a specific R&D department. There are two major tasks such a unit can have: supporting the business units and acting more long-term. The long-term aspect was mentioned by three of them.

One company stated clearly those two functions of their R&D unit. First, the business units focus more on current and next generations and improvements, while the R&D unit has a longer time horizon for its projects. Second, the R&D unit supports the business units. They also handle short-term activities which affect more than one business unit; thus not each business unit needs to do it separately. And they also support the business units in some other emergent cases.

One of the R&D units stated that it is part of their dedication to look ahead of the others and to recognise trends and innovations that eventually may be important for the whole company. Another one stated, as they provide the technology later used in the business units for product development, they need to think ahead and consider the market since their technology development needs longer time than the product development in the business units.

Yet not all R&D units are aiming at thinking more long-term. Especially one has its major purpose in supporting the business units by only reacting on their request. In that case they just act as a unit where the R&D knowledge is bundled and which provides its services.

Apart from a specific R&D unit, some companies split their portfolio into a research part and a development part, stated so by four companies. The former does the long-term activities, develops new technologies and runs pre-studies. The latter focuses on specific product development, deploying the outputs of the research portfolio. This separation enables them to manage these project types differently. The uncertain long-term research activities might have a less frequent portfolio reviews, another milestone process, and other criteria as more strategic and less financial focus.

As one company reported, their research and technology portfolio has much more projects but has much less money invested than their development portfolio, because the research portfolio consists of many small projects.

Yet this separation cannot solve all problems of course. One company, having a split between development projects and research, still remarked the difficulties in comparing the projects due to different size and lifecycle stage within each portfolio.

In principle, these approaches accord with the strategic buckets instrument.

Product areas with own profit responsibility

One company explained the important issues when separating the projects and products, accordingly to their product area, into different product units which are then responsible and measured each by its profit. There portfolio management is done separately in each unit. Each has few but large projects and products in different lifecycle stages. One product is just selling well on the market, being the cash cow, while the project for the next generation needs heavy R&D spending. The split between the areas must leave these units still being able to keep this balance within their portfolio. Otherwise, when having only investment cases and no cash cows, it can be a dedicated R&D unit, but not measured by profit. A desired balance between these independent units respectively product areas is kept by the management level above. And of course an overlap between the units needs to be avoided; thus the company has merged two units and portfolios respectively into one since the market development of their product areas had made them overlapping.

3.7.2 Standardisation

Since comparing projects and opportunities is an important part of portfolio management, it is important to keep the projects data comparable, thus standardised. The introduced playing cards respectively templates of Chapter 3.2.6, reported by two companies, are a consequent way for that; they present different projects which are open for discussion, each in the same compact form in order to ensure comparability.

As one company reported their cause for introducing a standardised way, "What we did in the past was that each of these product areas […] had their own responsibilities for running their project portfolio. So there have been individual ways of evaluating which projects we should run, and the decision process, and the performance management process, how to track progress of the projects. In some cases there has been a good structure. In other cases there has been very little follow-up in the projects. Overall it has been good because we have been able to launch a lot of successful products all the time. But we never had a good overview and the same way of working. So what we tried to do here is to get one way of working within the whole company. We have standard templates for project descriptions. And for follow-ups we have one template for tracking projects, status reports. We have one page with all the information, overview of each project, with description of the project, the expected financials. Then you have 3 areas: quality and cost, milestone timeline, and the top risk. We keep track of all these areas. [...] This is one way of standardising. Because in the past, basically, for each project there was one way of presenting the data and the studies. We couldn't compare different projects with each other."

Another company emphasised the importance of standardisation too, "Basically, maybe the tools we use are more template-like. So for instance we sort of standardised the playing cards and the project specification we have, try to formalise it in that way. More than mathematical processing or things like that."

3.7.3 Decisions locally or centrally

Two companies have partly shifted their decision competences from local areas to a central management.

One of them is already described in the previous section; they have introduced a standardised portfolio management across all product areas for having better overview. Along with that, the decision responsibility was transferred from these product areas to the central management. Now decisions are done centrally at the overall portfolio review. Status and milestone reviews still run locally in each product area; there are no decisions but it is rather a check if everything runs according to plan.

Another company had already established the milestone reviews and decisions on a higher, more central level for projects that are already quite advanced in their development. First, these projects need to occupy quite rare capacities in the company. And second, the higher management has a better overview how to set priorities in order to ensure proper market launches. But for projects in earlier stages, they were discussed and started only locally. Thus the central management got to know about them only at the later milestones. This often led to projects which, as central management then assessed, shouldn't have been started at all. Though it's a huge company, they now try to get central management also more involved in project starts. For project cancellation, in the early phase projects are mostly cancelled locally since they know better about their projects. Yet cancelling a later project definitely must be approved by the central management.

On the other hand, no company has reported any shift of responsibility from central management to local management.

3.7.4 Conclusion

From the portfolio perspective, specific R&D units are a mean of splitting the portfolio. Such units have the purposes to act more long-term than other units and to support other units. In some cases, they actively look ahead to long-term market trends and consequently prepare the technology.

There is a small tendency to shift the decisions from local sites to a more central, higher management level. For the benefits, central management has a better strategic overview and knowledge of company needs. And the central approach fosters the usage of a common portfolio management approach and thus provides better comparability and overall overview.

Determining at which hierarchy level decision-responsibility should be located seems tricky and maybe needs to be decided in each company out of past experience. It appears that splitting the portfolio according to different project types or areas is useful as it reduces each portfolio's size and allows adapted management processes for each. Nevertheless, projects, which compete for resources and thus need to be directly compared, should be tracked in a standardised way. And seemingly, important decisions and prioritisations are better done at higher management levels who keep overview about all R&D activities as well as the addressed customers.

Literature states similar aspects: Central management makes R&D better integrated in the overall business, while local one fosters faster decisions and better knowledge generation; see Chapter 2.10. Of course, the organisational aspect can be investigated in much more detail than this work intends to do; Chapter 1.2 shortly lists some further literature on this topic.

3.8 Allocating resources

The interviews had not been intended to elaborate on resourcing, yet have shown a few interesting issues. Hence, this chapter is not a comprehensive overview, but only a collection of resource-specific findings

One company, which has split up their portfolio into long-term research projects and specific product development projects, is still very flexible to shift resources in between. Then they set the priority on the product development projects because these have a fixed time schedule and a commitment to the customer when to deliver the product. Contrary, the research projects do not have any tight time schedule due to their high uncertainty. And although they are important, they are not urgent. Hence research is put backward when resources are short and needed for product development. To a certain extent the simple rule applies: product development gets what it needs; and what is left is spent on research. So resource spending across the project types varies from year to year and is pretty flexible. Of course, it makes it even harder to estimate how long a research project will take.

At its quarterly portfolio review, one company also thoroughly reviews the future resource situation of each project. They try to plan it ahead for the next year, consider all their available capacities and need to cope with looming bottlenecks. For instance, they can reveal where and when some work is planned, but no people assigned yet. Still they find it quite tricky to move people around within the organisation. Additionally, they deploy external consultancies in order to flexibly extend their people capacity.

One company has a quite special way of resource and result responsibility. The project management does not possess any resources but coordinates the line organisation. They ask the line organisation to provide the deliverables and results needed in the projects. Hence, it's the responsibility of the line organisation to deploy its resources properly in order to produce the demanded results. The benefit is that this way gives a very clear picture of responsibility for the results, the resources, and for solving any problems. Yet they also experience disadvantages. Since the project management only receives results from the line organisation, they don't know much about the resources there. Hence the project and portfolio management has difficulties to understand the overall resource situation, to recognise if too many projects are running already or if some resources are left for starting new ones. When portfolio management wants to start a new project, they regularly just start it. The resource situation rather reveals its troubles when doing the portfolio review.

Conclusion

The spending and planning of the resources can be kept more flexible by first planning them only for the product development projects, as they need to fulfil a time schedule and a customer commitment. Just the remaining resources are then used for the research projects, which are highly uncertain anyway und have no tight schedule.

For projects with lower uncertainty but a fairly complex organisation, it seems reasonable to plan months ahead when which resources will be needed. Thereby future bottlenecks can be recognised early and solved in a better way.

When the project managers do not own the resources for their projects but only order the deliveries from the line organisation, this provides a clearer responsibility for the results and resources. The drawback is that project managers hardly get an overview about the company's resource situation.

The interviews did not address resource allocation sufficiently for stating any connections to the literature approaches of Chapter 2.8.

3.9 Differentiation between product portfolio management and project portfolio management

Project portfolio management is tightly linked with product portfolio management as the projects are the future products. Moreover, a differentiation might appear tricky as all decisions about project selection and prioritisation are actually equal to deciding on which products to add. When defining project portfolio management as managing projects with strategic consideration as in Chapter 2.2, it clearly involves product portfolio management. In the same chapter, the separation of portfolio management into a strategic level and a tactical level includes product management with product roadmaps in the strategic level. Further, just the term portfolio management comprises products and projects – they are actually the same, but in different stages. In fact, one company has put everything in the same portfolio management, current projects as well as selling products.

Indeed, some companies forwarded my interview request for this topic to a department named product planning or similar. Especially large companies have another kind of separation between product portfolio management and project portfolio management, even located in different departments. One department is called product management, product planning or similar. This one is closer to the market, plans the products as well as the projects. In fact, the decisions are made there. The other department, maybe the development department itself, does the handling of the project portfolio. They rather execute what has been decided by the product department. Yet they are an important part of portfolio management too. They plan and decide on the resource allocation and the actual project execution. Obviously, both departments need to communicate intensively with each other.

3.10 Common challenges and problems

This chapter gathers some problems mentioned by the companies. Since I have not always asked about each single problem in the interviews but rather asked about any general worries companies experience, the fact that a company has not mentioned a problem may suggest that it is at least not an essential problem there, though could occur to a smaller extent. Therefore, the statements here should rather provide some qualitative comments, not show how many companies are concerned about a particular problem.

Strategy and keeping linked to it

The portfolio's link to strategy is not a large problem for the companies. None of them reported problems there.

One company which recently established a sophisticated portfolio management processes reported that they did so for still improving their strategy alignment. Further, as they were growing, they realised the need for better processes when the company exceeds a certain size.

Too many projects and too few resources

One of the most common problems in literature is having too many projects and too few resources, "So many projects for so little time." as one manager put it. Literature Chapter 2.3 considers avoiding too many projects even as a specific portfolio goal. A lapidary conclusion would say: Each company knows the problem; no one is really troubled by it.

The most positive attitude, when asked for this problem, was "I think it's a bigger problem if you have the other way round. So, yes, of course. But I think this is why we have processes to manage. [...] You can make bad decisions, and that happens all the time. You can make wrong decisions. But if you have a system in place, you have a mechanism to correct the bad decisions before they cause bigger damage. [...] But we always have of course a portfolio and a project planning, a project selection or selected projects portfolio which is larger than what we have ability to execute, always. So if we stop a project we always have some projects that were waiting for resources to be free. So having that situation, in a way I would say, is healthy because then you consider stopping a project on the merits of the projects itself. You don't think what is the point of stopping it, because otherwise what will the people do, so might we will continue. That's never the case, we always have more projects."

One company uses rather a classical funnel; many small studies are started which evolve to fewer larger projects. They argued that it is especially simple to start such a small, cheap study at the beginning; hence it's very typical to get too many projects easily. Apart from money, such research-based studies often require specifically experienced people who are pretty limited in the company. So they gradually try to cancel studies that don't appear attractive any more. Yet the rigorous decision is done rather later when the study either is blown up to a full project or cancelled.

Also another company reported often having too few experts in a certain area. Then they need to prioritise these projects which definitely need their expertise.

Some companies concluded that having too many projects has been more a problem in the past and has been pretty remedied by their newly introduced portfolio management processes. One of them just tries to limit the number of projects in the total portfolio to a certain number, whereas they count only the real projects lasting for several months, not the small activities.

Another company stated that they could reduce the number of projects by, basically, working in a more structured way and making the project decision more centralised where they have more overview. "I think that was a problem before more than it is today. I think if you look back ten years or so I think we started too many projects because we were not as experienced as we are today. We were not as good in assessing the risks. We didn't do it as structured as we do it today. So our local sides could take in projects that maybe shouldn't have been taken into the portfolio. And they were too weak, and they were in the portfolio forever. And there were still very few resources. So they got very few resources all of them. So all of them were standing there, not moving. So later on we have started to wipe out all these projects. What we want is to have a much more slimmed portfolio that is much more powerful and that can really progress." Today, they make project decisions in a rather centralised way, thus have more overview. Furthermore, they prioritise the projects and make better assessments for the risks.

There are external causes too, as one company reported. They are measured by a pretty high target for the number of released products, thus need many projects accordingly. There is somewhat the danger to make too many easy projects and products, just to meet the numbers. Yet they know that it's better to focus and still try to do so. "It's much more important to have a few really really really good interesting projects that eventually will make it than delivering a lot of okay but not very interesting stuff."

While one company considers itself pretty good in cancelling poor projects, they face another kind of resource challenge. As they are running few but large projects, mainly different generations of the same product line, there is always one project closest to the market release. Since this one, apparently, is the most urgent one, temptation is great to put too many resources on this project and, thereby, hurting the next one where the resources are taken from.

Two causes for having too many projects were reported by a company. First, they are organised in many smaller units, each basically responsible for a product line. There are somewhat too many units, already thinning out the money at this level, resulting in not enough money for each unit. Second, they are pretty overoptimistic when scheduling projects. They regularly take longer time and thus more resources. Yet they have also got much better with this than they had been in the past. Another positive effect might be that the projects tend to become larger in that branch. Contrary to the company above that easily starts many small studies, necessarily large expensive projects will easier prevent them from starting still one more when resources are already short.

Just having established a more sophisticated portfolio management process as shown in Chapter 4.1, one company experiences that they always have too many project ideas for the current year, while still having no plan what to do the next few years. So they try to plan the projects also further ahead for the next few years, leading to better long-term resource planning.

Concluding, companies have become better with starting only the number of projects they can properly resource. A systematic portfolio management seems to be helpful. And central decision-making, having more overview about all projects and resources, appears better than starting projects all around locally.

Feedback for R&D

The success of R&D is sometimes hard to measure, especially drawing a direct link to overall business success, although it might be the heart of a technology company.

Two companies discussed this issue. One R&D department reported that they hardly get feedback from their marketing units. Their products provide some additional features where the customers can select which ones to order. And it's an important decision in R&D which features to develop. So they would prefer more information about which products and which features the customers are buying, further how the customers are satisfied with them, and which features, once bought, they actually use.

Another R&D department acts basically as support on requests from the business divisions in the same company. They find it tricky to measure the results of their work for the customer divisions. They can only conclude, since their customers always come back and ask for more, that they probably are doing a good job. Yet they would desire a kind of key performance indicator for measuring their work in a better way.

This issue is somewhat recognised and tackled by literature as many articles investigate the collaboration and communication between marketing and R&D, as briefly mentioned in Chapter 1.2.

Cancelling projects at a late stage

One company reported the problem of cancelling projects at a late project stage when realising that its result or profit is lower than estimated. Then many resources have already been invested and are lost if cancelled now. Yet that investment is not to change any more. So they try to consider the remaining needed resources only and the – lower – benefit it will still deliver. If this gives a profit, they will continue. Even if they, of course, should not have started it in the first place.

In literature Chapter 2.4.1, net present value calculations like in Figure 2.2 might support by calculating the project value for different cases as early project cancellation, thus abandoning some remaining costs as well as earnings, and project continuation till end.

Apart from pure financial considerations, see Chapter 2.4.6. The more advanced forms of scoring tools, as Figure 2.6 and Figure 2.7, attempt to evaluate a project's performance and likelihood of success, depending on the current project stage. In the development stage, both figures state the cost criterion which is bad in this case. Yet they state also other criteria that should be considered too for project judgement.

Better long-term or easier short-term

One company talked about their tendency to favour short-term projects. Actually, they want to have a certain part of the portfolio with a very long-term perspective. But this comes into conflict when resources are scarce; then there is always a tendency to take the projects with quicker earnings. Usually, top management wants to keep the long-term ones, while middle management wants to abandon them and do the short-term activities instead.

An R&D department, supporting the business divisions within the same company on their request, said that these customer divisions sometimes rather ask for support in daily work activities. Yet its dedication is to do R&D work and provide competences that do only exist in the R&D unit. There is the danger of getting stuck in short-term daily work; so they have to take care of this and prioritise the requests properly.

Understanding the own capacities

One company reported that one of the largest problems closely related to the projects is capacity planning. There are many people in many different competence areas who will work on a project at different times. "One very important piece of our work is to understand ourselves of what we can do. Now and in 3 months and in 6 months and in 12 months. So to understand the capacity in an R&D organisation." So they want to utilise their resources efficiently, yet not overload it with more than what they can cope with. As each development project is new and different, it's even trickier. Along with that, they consider cooperation and coordination as another major challenge. There tools can help; yet it more depends on the people and how clearly they communicate.

Flexibility for market changes

One company reported that their market is quite fast-moving and thus requires them to be very flexible. They are forced to make many adaptations to the projects, often also in the late stages where it is especially tricky. Yet too many changes make them inefficient, they actually could perform better without so much changing. So they need to find the right degree and trade-off of flexibility.

Overestimating the projects' results

One company said that they regularly tend to overestimate the future advantages of a project when assessing and starting it. Now they try to look back to past projects. If there never was a project achieving such a high step, it's unlikely that the current project will do. So this helps for making more realistic estimations about future projects.

4 Notable overall company methods

Many ideas of the companies have already been presented in the previous chapters. Here three companies with a pretty interesting overall portfolio management are introduced.

4.1 Filling up intended levels of future revenues and R&D costs

This company wanted to move completely away from the classical portfolio management as a bottom-up approach where the best ideas are selected in a funnel-like system. Their idea for another kind of management

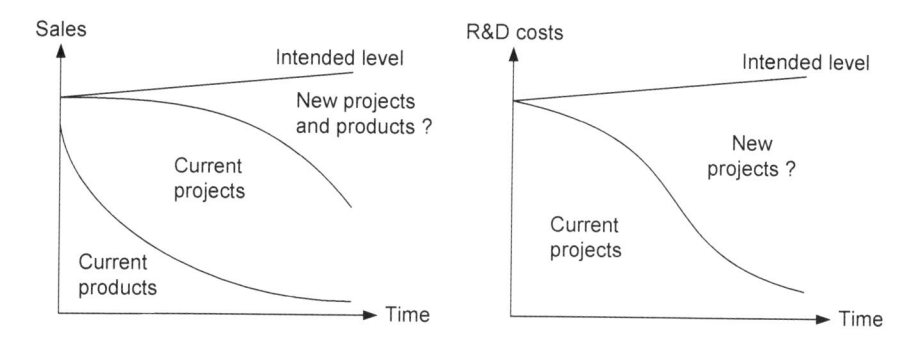

Figure 4.1 Achieving future sales and R&D costs

approach mainly was induced by one question: Is it a good portfolio which we currently have? They realised that they couldn't answer without having defined where their portfolio actually should take them.

Now they start as a top-down approach. They define where they want to be in the future, which businesses, which countries, and which segments. Further they forecast and determine their intended levels of sales and R&D costs for the next years, as shown in Figure 4.1. These levels should stay constant or even slightly rise as growth is mostly desired. For sales, at the moment – at the beginning of the time axis – the currently selling products gain high sales. However, they will become old and their sales will shrink over the next years. Then there are the current development projects which soon will be launched as products and bring new sales. For R&D costs, the intended spending goes to these current projects at the moment. Yet spending on these projects will shrink when they are finished and start selling; and later also their sales will decline when they become obsolete in the market. Then, on the sales side, they need new projects that will become selling products. And for R&D, there are still resources available in the future for investing in such new projects. Obviously, this approach considers everything in one large portfolio, consisting of the currently selling products, the currently ongoing projects, and the future opportunities not being projects yet.

These forecasts of sales and R&D spending seem tricky and uncertain. However, basically, rough estimations are sufficient for this calculation. And of course, everybody needs to be aware that these are just estimations. Moreover, they have quite many projects and have experienced that, indeed, the overall estimations deliver pretty well results as the project deviations – one too low estimated, another one too high – somehow compensate each other. And as they come closer in time and more current projects and products go into the calculations, the figures get better.

At the beginning, this new approach was used together with some traditional tools as matrix charts and so on. But they have removed them by now as nobody felt confident in using them.

New ideas

Also in a top-down approach, they face the tricky part of finding new future opportunities. They need new ideas and projects to fill their gap between the intended level and the current projects and products. By this way, the model, in fact, shows the needed amount of new opportunities.

However, the new opportunities are mainly found by doing market research and by having ideas what to deliver to the customers. Then technical idea searching should be focused on these areas. Ideas, whatever great and innovative, which do not match the strategy are abandoned as the will not find a market and customers. For the technical part, this company's branch and products do not require outstanding research. They rather do kind of product development where they can fairly rely on achieving their technical targets. So referring to the classification of Chapter 3.6, this company is clearly development-based and starts with the strategy.

Finally, the results of the identified new opportunities need to be quantified in terms of time and money and get filled into the model. "We need to fill that future business. We need to fill the gaps. This is more straight forward. I mean we still put all the thought process into what those opportunities should be. And we still do all the consumer insight, and all the creativity, and all the technology development and so on. But it's based more on a top-down approach, rather than just a big bottom-up."

Advantages

The major advantages of this top-down approach are, first, that it allows long-term planning and, second, the tight link between strategy and projects.

The new model gives answer whether the portfolio can sustain the planned business the next years. When coming wrong – maybe also due to inadequate estimations –, they can early recognise it and react.

Long-term planning enables them to know future resource spending well in advance. Thus they can plan their resources long-term instead of just reacting when a new project gets started and demands resources immediately.

At any time the model contains the current products, ongoing projects, and the future opportunities. It makes obvious that, when cancelling a project from the R&D cost side, it is cancelled from the sales side too, maybe leaving a gap that needs to be filled with new a project in order to achieve the sales target.

Limitations

The company itself admits that this approach fits for them, not for everybody. They need to maintain a stable flow of innovation in their product lines and need to know what they want to launch in the market. But they are not research-based and act in a rather easy product development. For high-uncertainty R&D, such financial forecasts might prove unreasonable.

4.2 Sophisticated strategic buckets

This company has established a pretty well-structured management approach. They have set goals for the portfolio, categorised the portfolio by strategic buckets into three main groups, and applied different practices in each group fitting best for the specific project type.

Figure 4.2 depicts this structure. By strategic buckets, the whole portfolio is spilt into three different groups, each having a defined fairly constant share of the total R&D spending assigned. These are product development, product maintenance, and research. A yearly portfolio review is done for the total portfolio.

Research, definitely applied research, contains pretty long-term projects lasting for several years. At the portfolio review, the current ones are reviewed and new ones to add are decided. The focus where to do research is pretty steered by the strategic focus.

Product maintenance runs small, short-term projects. They are also reviewed at the yearly portfolio review. However, as these projects regularly are shorter than one year, they cannot be decided only yearly. Hence at the yearly meeting, only the budget is decided. And within this budget frame, projects are started throughout the year. Furthermore, this bucket is spilt further into three sub-buckets, being cost reductions, quality improvements, and product adjustments. At cost reduction, there is a simple ranking list considering basically the payback time of a cost reduction project. Product adjustments are small adjustments, for instance when an existing product should be introduced into a new market. There a ranking is created by a simple scoring instrument with a few criteria, deciding which ones to do first.

Portfolio goals:
Strategy alignment, profitability, balance

Product development, medium-term, project start decisions at yearly review	
Feature improvements Feature targets tool Monthly gathered milestone reviews	**Completely new products**

Product maintenance, short-term, project start decisions during the year		
Cost reductions Ranking list	**Quality improvements**	**Product adjustments** Ranking list

Research, long-term, project start decisions at yearly review

Figure 4.2 Strategic buckets, with adapted projects handling in each bucket (graph's proportions not necessarily true)

Finally, product development is the portfolio's major part. Here runs the real product development. The projects are medium-term. The yearly portfolio review decides which projects to add. A further split categorises feature improvements and completely new products, framing the former as the major part. Of course new products will use the improved features too. Feature improvements attempt to improve the product feature as mainly stated by strategy. Therefore, they deploy the feature target instrument as introduced in Chapter 3.2.5. Each feature has a roadmap and the specific assigned projects for achieving the feature target. In case of too many projects, they can prioritise by the importance of the features. Each month a few project milestones pile up which are reviewed together at a monthly meeting. There, as a few projects are reviewed and their deviations need to be coped with, it somewhat becomes a monthly small portfolio review.

The total portfolio has three goals, being strategy alignment, profitability, and balance. Strategy alignment is mainly pursued by the feature target instrument. There each feature is defined according to strategy; and each project strives for a feature. Profitability, again mainly addressed by the product development bucket, is aimed at by checking each project for a certain minimum profitability when deciding about to start at. Less profitably projects may happen for strategic reasons of course. Balance, finally, is achieved with the complete strategic buckets system.

Advantages

As the feature instrument is the heart of this approach, this instrument's advantages benefit here too. It is control over the situation of reaching the strategic features of the products. Some years ago, they did neither that monthly review nor had a system for measuring the features. Only at the yearly review, they worked through where the stood in each project and realised, eventually, where the targets were slipping.

They consider the feature system as more sophisticated than rankings. Ranking is only applied for the small short-term project. "But not on the big ones, because then it's more important that you follow the feature strategy than anything else."

Also for this company, they emphasise strategy focus. If they have a good idea with possibility to improve features, they will start a project based on that. However, it must correspond with what strategy intends for the features. And applied research is directed only to certain focused areas, which is quite new; before rather the creativity of ideas had given the direction.

The strategic buckets according to project time horizon maintain the balance and enable to apply different adjusted processes in each bucket.

Limitations

This company has pretty many projects. For a smaller portfolio, it might prove unreasonable to split it in buckets and even sub-buckets.

As an attribute of the feature target instrument, they might be tricky to apply to some other kinds of products.

And as discussed in Chapter 3.6, the strict alignment to product strategy is not possible in all branches.

4.3 Assessing the project value in research

The following approach is of a company whose projects are pretty research-based. Yet they directly address a market for their developed technologies.

This research company typically acts as stated in Chapter 3.6. Their major approach is not the definition of certain customers and thus the needed products and projects, even if they have a broad strategy where and how they want to go and how to address customers of course. Yet here an important approach is to get an idea and to evaluate it whether it makes sense to pursue it further.

They have five project areas which, in the past, were managing their portfolios in different ways. Looking at the result, it actually was doing quite well; nevertheless, the never got a really overview about their whole company situation. Now they have introduced one standardised system for all areas. Some of their methods have already been mentioned in previous chapters.

A major part is a matrix diagram for categorising the projects, showing a project's EBIT potential on one axis and its risk level on the other. Basically, they try to keep balance there. Still they find it difficult to find high-EBIT-potential, low-risk projects. And they are aware that the diagram does not show everything; some projects might look bad there yet are good and important ones due to other reasons. They have also tried some other parameters on the axis instead of EBIT, but have found it too complicate. They reported that they want to keep it as simple as possible for the decision makers to understand easily why they should base their decisions on these instruments. And after all, earnings remain a central aspect.

Another major part is to select new ideas. There is another matrix diagram, showing on the axes the value for the customer and the fit for the company respectively. Company fit, basically, is in terms of technology, production and so on. This diagram is used for an initial screening of the ideas since they regularly have more ideas than they actually can do projects. Of course, they try to pick the high-customer-value, high-company-fit ideas. Interesting ideas are assessed further. Then it becomes kind of a business case with deeper analysis, financial figures and so on. There they also evaluate the figures needed for the first diagram as the expected EBIT potential and the risk level.

Each project is described on a standardised template, mainly for keeping track on ongoing ones. One page gives the basic overview and information with a description and financial figures. Further it shows the three issues where they want to keep track on: quality and costs, milestone schedule, and risk.

There is no ranking through the portfolio, but each project gets a certain priority stage. There is top priority, normal priority, and an on-hold stage for continuing maybe in the future.

The portfolio review is done twice a year for the whole company. Each project is looked at. Projects without much progress since the previous review are questioned. And here they do the decisions about starting new projects and cancelling or changing existing ones. Locally at each product area, there are a monthly portfolio review and the project milestone reviews.

Yet no decisions are done there since portfolio management now should be done together for the whole company. The local reviews are only for tracking the progress whether everything goes as planned and for approving that a milestone is reached.

Before starting a project, they attempt to secure the necessary resources. That is in order to avoid having more projects than they actually can resource. Further they have defined a rough number of projects that should no be exceeded in the portfolio.

Advantages

Screening new projects for their value for the customer as well as their fit for the own company is useful to initially assess the ideas. Eventually such ideas will become new products. This appears pretty beneficial in their research-branch where it is not possible to let the technology just follow what has been defined as markets and products.

They have shifted the decisions to the central management as well as have established thoroughly a standardised way. This provides more overview about which projects are running in the company and to keep track on them.

Limitations

In other branches that are technologically easier but have a tough market to address, this market orientation might not be strong enough.

5 Conclusions

Research review

This work aims at, first, presenting the literature's status and descriptions on how to manage an R&D portfolio and, second, revealing some practical experiences of R&D project portfolio management and explaining the reasons why companies have adopted just their way of working and not another one.

For the first aim, many authors investigate this topic. They hardly contradict each other. Yet they view it from pretty different perspectives, start at different points, and emphasis different factors; this could make it somewhat confusing when just reading through my literature chapter as a manual for practitioners.

For the second aim, the questions how and why might seem clear, yet are somewhat fuzzy in the face of the wide range of interrelated issues within this broad topic. Thus my work cannot claim to cover every aspect and to cover the whole topic evenly. Moreover, it seems that among the companies, each has different aspects that are important, challenging, or troublesome. Worse, the reasons sometimes can only be given by my interpretation. This is because, first, when working through the recorded interviews, some interesting insights emerged for me which I had not been thinking to address before in the interviews; and second, in many companies the way of working has evolved over years, eventually ending up with a way of working that seems good, yet without any explicit reason. Moreover, the number of interviewed companies is rather small, and they even are a mixture of various industry branches – the latter has broadened the spectrum of findings, yet both together cause the need for further research to confirm my findings. Nevertheless, I present two hypotheses about the overall portfolio management approach and plenty of interesting insights.

Insights

Hypothesis: Companies and departments respectively, which directly face a market with less customer-binding and less customised products, develop a more sophisticated project and product portfolio management approach. Contrary, those, which have high binding with internal or external customers and develop customised products for them, have a less sophisticated project and product portfolio management, because their portfolio management is dominated by customer alignment. While there is much literature that investigates best practice, which could be used to define my term of a sophisticated portfolio management more precisely, I have not found any literature investigating this dependence on the market and customer situation.

Hypothesis: The more the projects belong to research and thus face more technical uncertainty, the more these companies and departments respectively just assess the value of ideas rather than strive for a strict strategy alignment at their project selection. Contrary, the more the projects belong to product development with less technical uncertainty, the more these companies respectively departments introduce an approach that is stronger directed towards strategy and markets. While a considerable part of the literature investigates such different types of projects as well as their individual handling and thus could be used for further research, I have not found any literature investigating the influence of the project types on the overall approach of project selection.

Regarding portfolio goals, companies mostly strive for a kind of strategy or delivering customer value and, sometimes along with that, for a certain sufficient portfolio output and delivery. While individual projects also are evaluated using financial figures, financial portfolio goals are rarely used, presumably due to the uncertainty of such numbers. Many companies strive for some kind of portfolio balance.

When selecting projects, no company can ignore money and thus financial estimations. Yet uncertainty and even different degrees of uncertainty across the projects make it somewhat unreliable for comparing projects. Therefore, some broad numbers from experience are used rather than individual, precise calculations that might fail anyway. Some companies use scoring tools, but only with pretty simply configurations. No company makes use of the more advanced scoring tools and models of the literature. The resulting scores are used for rankings, while they definitely are reviewed and maybe re-prioritised by people. Diagrams are used for quickly showing some aspects of the portfolio. Yet rarely are they used in a systematic way and as major part of decision making, as they only show small aspects and do not state clear results. Strategic buckets are mostly used to split product areas and sometimes for different project types and time horizons. Such a balance in terms of time horizon and risk even can be achieved by a separate R&D unit, dedicated to the long-term projects.

The feature target tool, used by companies, is unknown in current literature as I have found. Thereby, a number of strategically important product features are defined, together with a target at which future time to reach which level of the feature. Each feature has a roadmap assigned to it, mapping the individual projects working on this feature. The benefits are that each project is assigned to a strategically important feature, product features can be better forecasted, further it gives clear decision support where projects are needed and where not, and it suggests project priorities according to the feature priorities.

Generally about instruments, no company binds its decisions to instrument outcomes. They merely are taken as information aspects and assistance. It's important for managers to understand and evaluate the meaning of the real projects behind some tools' results. Further, companies tend to standardise their project descriptions to make them more convenient to compare. Apart from providing information, I have found the aspect of even moderating the discussion by tools. For instance, the happening of giving scoring points for several projects fosters that all people truly start thinking and opinion-making about the projects. So instruments even incite thinking and discussing, not replace it.

Companies choose projects which satisfy strategy and customer requirements, and besides bring money. The instruments used are wished to support this view in a simple and straightforward way, without too much modelling in between. First, complex calculations might fail anyway because of uncertainty. And second, apparently people truly want to understand and think through what they decide and do. Therefore, whichever perfect portfolios a tool could create, it must feel simple and straight if it should get adopted in practice. The feature targets tool, emerged in practice, is a fine example for that.

At the large portfolio review, most companies review each project thoroughly, as this seemingly provides a more comfortable way to get a real overview about the portfolio than considering only aggregated data. Additionally, some companies have introduced extra reviews, being more frequent but smaller. Often monthly and sometimes being a mixture between a portfolio review and a project milestone review, these reviews aim at keeping better track of the projects, for instance for the most important projects or at the local operative sites. The large portfolio review is the major meeting for decisions, yet some companies have further specific project selection meetings.

All companies use a gate process for individual projects. At the gates, many companies consider both whether the previous work was done properly and fulfils the criteria and specifications, and the project's future prospects and priority in the portfolio. The specific milestone, which is the transaction from the cheaper pre-study, evaluation, and business-case-forming phase to the expensive development phase, is indeed handled as a major decision step in most companies. One company attempts to overlap the project stages by starting the next project stage before the current one is finished. They have found that being faster is much more valuable than the more of imposed risk.

There is a small tendency to shift decision making from local sites to a more central management. Centrally, they have more overview about the whole company situation and strategy. Thereby, they also foster a more standardised way of portfolio management and thus better project comparability. However, the task of just keeping track of the projects without big decisions can stay locally.

The major challenges the companies have named are quite various. They are about understanding the own capacities when doing resource planning some time ahead, the lack of feedback about their R&D work, the right degree of flexibility for reacting to changing market demands, overestimating the projects' impacts, and deciding on project cancellation at a late project stage. The common problem of running too many projects with too few resources is known amongst all companies; yet they tend to handle this better than in the past and are not seriously troubled by that. A more structured and formalised and partly more centralised way of decision-making appears helpful for not allowing too many projects being started.

6 Literature

Albright, Richard E./Kappel, Thomas A. (2003): Roadmapping in the Corporation. In Research Technology Management, March-April 2003, p. 31-40.

Amabile, Teresa M. (1998): How To Kill Creativity. In: Harvard Business Review, September-October 1998, p. 77-87.

Archer, Norm/Ghasemzadeh (1999): An integrated framework for project portfolio selection. In: International Journal of Project Management, Vol. 17, No. 4, p. 207-216.

Baker, Norman R. (1974): R & D Project Selection Models: An Assessment. In: IEEE Transactions on Engineering Management, Vol. EM-21, No. 4, p. 165-171.

Balachandra, R./Friar, John H. (1997): Factors for Success in R&D Projects and New Product Innovation: A Contextual Framework. In: IEEE Transactions on Engineering Management, Vol. 44, No. 3, p. 276-287.

Bard, Jonathan F./Balachandra, Ramaiya/Kaufmann, Pedro E. (1988): An Interactive Approach to R&D Project Selection and Termination. In: IEEE Transactions on Engineering Management, Vol. 35, No. 3, p. 139-146.

Bart, Christopher K. (1988): Organizing for New Product Development. In: The Journal of Business Strategy, July/August 1988, p. 34-38.

Bellmann, Matthias/Schaffer, Robert H. (2001): Freeing Managers to Innovate. In: Harvard Business Review, June 2001, p. 32-33.

Brown, Shona L./Eisenhardt, Kathleen M. (1995): Product Development: Past Research, Present Findings, and Future Directions. In: Academy of Management Review, Vol. 20, No. 2, p. 343-378.

Calantone, Roger J./Di Benedetto, C. Anthony/Schmidt, Jeffrey B. (1999): Using the Analytic Hierarchy Process in New Product Screening. In: Journal of Product Innovation Management, Vol. 16, p. 65-76.

Cook-Davies, Terry (2002): The "real" success factors on projects. In: International Journal of Project Management, Vol. 20, p. 185-190.

Cooper, Robert G./Kleinschmidt, Elko J. (1986): An Investigation into the New Product Process: Steps, Deficiencies, and Impact. In: Journal of Product Innovation Management, Vol. 3, p. 71-85.

Cooper, Robert G. (1992): The NewProd System: The Industry Experience. In: Journal of Product Innovation Management, Vol. 9, p. 113-127.

Cooper, Robert G./Kleinschmidt, Elko J. (1995a): Benchmarking Firms' New Product Performance & Practices. In: IEEE Engineering Management Review, Vol. 23, No. 3, p. 112-120.

Cooper, Robert G./Kleinschmidt, Elko J. (1995b): Benchmarking the Firm's Critical Success Factors in New Product Development. In: Journal of Product Innovation Management, Vol. 12, p. 374-391.

Cooper, Robert G./Kleinschmidt, Elko J. (1996): Winning Business in Product Development: The Critical Success Factors. In: Research Technology Management, Vol. 39, No. 4, p. 18-29.

Cooper, Robert G./Edgett, Scott J./Kleinschmidt, Elko J. (1997a): Portfolio Management in New Product Development: Lessons from the Leaders – I. In: Research Technology Management, Vol. 40, No. 5, p. 16-28.

Cooper, Robert G./Edgett, Scott J./Kleinschmidt, Elko J. (1997b): Portfolio Management in New Product Development: Lessons from the Leaders – II. In: Research Technology Management, Vol. 40, No. 6, p. 43-52.

Cooper, Robert G./Edgett, Scott J./Kleinschmidt, Elko J. (1998): Best Practices for Managing R&D Portfolios. In: Research Technology Management, Vol. 41, No. 4, p. 20-33.

Cooper, Robert G. (1999): From Experience: The Invisible Success Factors in Product Innovation. In: Journal of Product Innovation Management, Vol. 16, p. 115-133.

Cooper, Robert G./Edgett, Scott J./Kleinschmidt, Elko J. (1999): New Product Portfolio Management: Practices and Performances. In: Journal of Product Innovation Management, Vol. 16, p. 333-351.

Cooper, Robert G./Edgett, Scott J./Kleinschmidt, Elko J. (2000): New Problems, New Solutions: Making Portfolio Management More Effective. In: Research Technology Management, Vol. 43, No. 2, p. 18-33.

Cooper, Robert G./Edgett, Scott J./Kleinschmidt, Elko J. (2001): Portfolio Management for New Product Development: Results of an Industry Practices Study. In: R&D Management, Vol. 31, No. 4, p. 361-380.

Cooper, Robert G./Edgett, Scott J./Kleinschmidt, Elko J. (2002a): Optimizing the Stage-Gate Process: What Best-Practice Companies Do—I. In: Research Technology Management, Vol. 45, No. 5, p. 21-27.

Cooper, Robert G./Edgett, Scott J./Kleinschmidt, Elko J. (2002b): Optimizing the Stage-Gate Process: What Best-Practice Companies Do—II. In: Research Technology Management, Vol. 45, No. 6, p. 43-49.

Cooper, Robert G./Edgett, Scott J. (2003): Overcoming the Crunch in Resources for New Product Development. In: Research Technology Management, May-June 2003, p. 48-58.

Cooper, Robert G./Edgett, Scott J./Kleinschmidt, Elko J. (2004a): Benchmark Best NPD Practices—I. In: Research Technology Management, Vol. 47, No. 1, p. 31-43.

Cooper, Robert G./Edgett, Scott J./Kleinschmidt, Elko J. (2004b): Benchmark Best NPD Practices—II. In: Research Technology Management, Vol. 47, No. 3, p. 50-59.

Cooper, Robert G./Edgett, Scott J./Kleinschmidt, Elko J. (2004c): Benchmark Best NPD Practices—III. In: Research Technology Management, Vol. 47, No. 6, p. 43-55.

Cooper, Robert G. (2005): Product Leadership : Pathways to Profitable Innovation. Basic Books.

Cormican, Kathryn/O'Sullivan, David (2004): Auditing best practice for effective product innovation management. In: Technovation, Vol. 24, No. 10, 819-829.

Danilovic, Mike/Sandkull, Bengt (2005): The use of dependence structure matrix and domain mapping matrix in managing uncertainty in multiple project situations. In: International Journal of Project Management, Vol. 23, p. 193-203.

Danneels, Erwin/Kleinschmidt, Elko J. (2001): Product innovativeness from the firm's perspective: Its dimensions and their relation with project selection and performance. In: Journal of Product Innovation Management, Vol. 18, p. 357-373.

Davidson, Jeffrey M./Clamen, Allen/Karol, Robin A. (1999): Learning from the Best New Product Developers. In: Research Technology Management, Vol. 42, No. 4, p. 12-18.

De Maio, Adriano/Verganti, Roberto/Corso, Mariano (1994): A multi-project management framework for new product development. In: European Journal of Operational Research, Vol. 78, No. 2, p. 178-191.

Dewar, Robert D./Dutton, Jane E. (1986): The Adoption of Radical and Incremental Innovations: An Empirical Analysis. In: Management Science, Vol. 32, No. 11, p. 1422-1433.

Dietrich, Perttu/Lehtonen, Päivi (2005): Successful management of strategic intentions through multi projects – Reflections from empirical study. In: International Journal of Project Management, Vol. 23, p. 386-391.

Dooley, Kevin J./Subra, Anand/Anderson, John (2002): Adoption Rates and Patterns of Best Practices in New Product Development. In: International Journal of Innovation Management, Vol. 6, No. 1, p. 85-103.

Dvir, D./Lipovetsky, S./Shenhar, A/Tishler, A. (1998): In search of project classification: a non-universal approach to project success factors. In: Research Policy, Vol. 27, p. 915-935.

Elonen, Suvi/Artto, Karlos A. (2003): Problems in managing internal development projects in multi-project environments. In: International Journal of Project Management, Vol. 21, p. 395-402.

Englund, Randall L./Graham, Robert J. (1999): From Experience: Linking Projects to Strategy. In: Journal of Product Innovation Management, Vol. 16, p. 52-64.

Engwall, Mats (2003): No project is an island: linking projects to history and context. In: Research Policy, Vol. 32, p. 789-808.

Engwall, Mats/Jerbrant, Anna (2003): The resource allocation syndrome: the prime challenge of multi-project management? In: International Journal of Project Management, Vol. 21, p. 403-409.

Eskerod, Pernille (1996): Meaning and action in a multi-project environment. In: International Journal of Project Management, Vol. 14, No. 2, p. 61-65.

Ettlie, John E./Bridges, William P./O'Keefe, Robert D. (1984): Organization Strategy and Structural Differences for Radical versus Incremental Innovation. In: Management Science, Vol. 30, No. 6, p. 682-695.

Ferns, D. C. (1991): Developments in programme management. In: International Journal of Project Management, Vol. 9, No. 3, p. 148-156.

Fricke, Scott E./Shenhar, Aaron J. (2000): Managing Multiple Engineering Projects in a Manufacturing Support Environment. In: IEEE Transactions on Engineering Management, Vol. 47, No. 2, p. 258-268.

Frumerman, Robert/Cicero, Daniel/Baetens, Charles (1987a): R&D Programs with Multiple Related Projects – I. In: Research Management, Vol. 30, No. 5, p. 31-35.

Frumerman, Robert/Cicero, Daniel/Baetens, Charles (1987b): R&D Programs with Multiple Related Projects – II. In: Research Management, Vol. 30, No. 6, p. 40-44.

Granot, Daniel/Zuckerman, Dror (1991): Optimal Sequencing and resource Allocation in Research and Development Projects. In: Management Science, Vol. 37, No. 2, p. 140-156.

Graves, Samuel B./Ringuest, Jeffrey L./Case, Randolph H. (2000): Formulating Optimal R&D Portfolios. In: Research Technology Management, Vol. 43, No. 3, p. 47-51.

Gray, Roderic J. (1996): Alternative approaches to programme management. In: International Journal of Project Management, Vol. 15, No. 1, p. 5-9.

Gray, R. J./Bamford, P. J. (1999): Issues in programme integration. In: International Journal of Project Management, Vol. 17, No. 6, p. 361-366.

Griffin, Abbie/Page, Albert L. (1993): An Interim Report on Measuring Product Development Success and Failure. In: Journal of Production Innovation Management, Vol. 10, p. 291-308.

Griffin, Abbie/Hauser, John R. (1996): Integrating R&D and Marketing: A Review and Analysis of the Literature. In: Journal of Production Innovation Management, Vol. 13, p. 191-215.

Griffin, Abbie (1997): PDMA Research on New Product Development Practices: Updating Trends and Benchmarking Best Practices. In: Journal of Product Innovation Management, Vol. 14, p. 429-458.

Hall, David/Nauda, Alexander (1990): An Interactive Approach for Selecting IR&D Projects. In: IEEE Transactions on Engineering Management, Vol. 37, No. 2, p. 126-133.

Hart, Susan/Tzokas, Nikolaos/Saren, Michael (1999): The effectiveness of market information in enhancing new product success rates. In: European Journal of Innovation Management, Vol. 2, No. 1, p. 20-35.

Hendriks, Martien H. A./Voeten, Bas/Kroep, Leon H. (1999): Human resource allocation in a multi-project R&D environment. In: International Journal of Project Management, Vol. 17, No. 3, p. 181-188.

Henriksen, Anne DePiante/Traynor, Ann Jensen (1999): A Practical R&D Project-Selection Scoring Tool. In: IEEE Transactions on Engineering Management, Vol. 46, No. 2, p. 158-170.

Jackson, Byron (1983): Decision Methods for Selecting a Portfolio of R&D Projects. In: Research Management, September-Oktocer 1983, p. 21-26.

Kahn, Arshad M./Fiorino, Donald P. (1992): The Capital Asset Pricing Model in Project Selection: A Case Study. In: The Engineering Economist, Vol. 37, No. 2, p. 145-160.

Kahn, Kenneth B./Barczak, Gloria/Moss, Roberta (2006): Perspective: Establishing an NPD Best Practices Framework. In: Journal of Product Innovation Management, Vol. 23, p. 106-116.

Keegan, Anne/Turner, J. Rodney (2002): The Management of Innovation in Project-Based Firms. In: Long Range Planning, Vol. 35, p. 367-388.

Krogh, Lester C./Prager, Julianne H./Sorensen, David P./Tomlinson, John D. (1988): How 3M Evaluates its R&D Programs. In: Research Technology Management, Vol. 31, No. 6, p. 10-14.

Kumar, Vinod/Persaud, Aditha N. S./Kumar, Uma (1996): To Terminate or Not an Ongoing R&D Project: A Managerial Dilemma. In: IEEE Transactions on Engineering Management, Vol. 43, No. 3, p. 273-284.

Loch, Christoph (2000): Tailoring Product Development to Strategy: Case of a European Technology Manufacturer. In: European Management Journal, Vol. 18, No. 3, p. 246-258.

Lycett, Mark/Rassau, Andreas/Danson, John (2004): Programme management: a critical review. In: International Journal of Project Management, Vol. 22, p. 289-299.

Matheson, David/Matheson, James E./Menke, Michael M. (1994): Making Excellent R&D Decisions. In: Research Technology Management, Vol. 37, No. 6, p. 21-24.

Matheson, James E./Menke, Michael M. (1994): Using Decision Quality Principles To Balance Your R&D Portfolio. In: Research Technology Management, Vol. 37, No. 3, p. 38-43.

McDonough III, Edward F./Spital, Francis C. (2003): Managing Project Portfolios. In: Research Technology Management, Vol. 46, No. 3, p. 40-46.

McQuater, R. E./Peters, A. J./Dale, B. G./Spring, M./Rogerson, J. H./Rooney, E. M. (1998): The management and organisational context of new product development: Diagnosis and self-assessment. In: International Journal of Production Economics, Vol. 55, p. 121-131.

Menke, Michael M. (1997a): Essentials of R&D Strategic Excellence. In: Research Technology Management, Vol. 40, No. 5, p. 42-47.

Menke, Michael M. (1997b): Managing R&D for Competitive Advantage. In: Research Technology Management, Vol. 40, No. 6, p. 40-42.

Meyer, Marc H./Tertzakian, Peter/Utterback, James M. (1997): Metrics for Managing Research and Development in the Context of the Product Family. In Management Science, Vol. 43, No. 1, p. 88-111.

Moenaert, Rudy K./Souder, William E. (1990): An Information Transfer Model for Integrating Marketing and R&D Personnel in New Product Development Project. In: Journal of Product Innovation Management, Vol. 7, p. 91-107.

Montoya-Weiss, Mitzi M./Calantone, Roger (1994): Determinants of New Product Performance: A Review and Meta-Analysis. In: Journal of Product Innovation Management, Vol. 11, p. 397-417.

Nobelius, D. (2004): Towards the sixth generation of R&D management. In: International Journal of Project Management, Vol. 22, p. 369-375.

Nobeoka, Kentaro/Cusumano, Michael A. (1997): Multiproject Strategy and Sales Growth: The Benefits of Rapid Design Transfer in New Product Development. In: Strategic Management Journal, Vol. 18, No. 3, p. 169-186.

Nohria, Nitin/Gulati, Ranjay (1996): Is Slack Good or Bad For Innovation? In: The Academy of Management Journal, Vol. 39, No. 5, p. 1245-1264.

Page, Albert L. (1993): Assessing New Product Development Practices and Performance: Establishing Crucial Norms. In: Journal of Product Innovation Management, Vol. 10, p. 273-290.

Patterson, Marvin L. (1998): From Experience: Linking Product Innovation to Business Growth. In: Journal of Product Innovation Management, Vol. 15, p. 390-402.

Payne, John H. (1995): Management of multiple simultaneous projects: a state-of-the-art review. In: International Journal of Project Management, Vol. 13, No. 3, p. 163-168.

Payne, John H./Turner, J. Rodney (1999): Company-wide project management: the planning and control of programmes of projects of different type. In: International Journal of Project Management, Vol. 17, No. 1, p. 55-59.

Pellegrinelli, Sergio (1997): Programme management: organising project-based change. In: International Journal of Project Management, Vol. 15, No. 3, p. 141-149.

Pillai, A. Sivathanu/Joshi, A./Rao, K. Srinivasa (2002): Performance measurement of R&D projects in a multi-project, concurrent engineering environment. In: International Journal of Project Management, Vol. 20, p. 165-177.

Platje, A./Seidel, H. (1993): Breakthrough in multiproject management: how to escape the vicious circle of planning and control. In: International Journal of Project Management, Vol. 11, No. 4, p. 209-213.

Platje, Adri/Seidel, Harald/Wadman, Sipke (1994): Project and portfolio planning cylce. In: International Journal of Project Management, Vol. 12, No. 2, p. 100-106.

Poolton, Jenny/Barclay, Ian (1998): New Product Development From Past Research to Future Applications. In: Industrial Marketing Management, Vol. 27, p. 197-212.

Rice, Mark P./O'Connor, Gina Colarelli/Peters, Lois S./Morone, Joseph G. (1998): Managing Discontinuous Innovation. In: Research Technology Management, Vol. 41, No. 3, p. 52-58.

Ringuest, Jeffrey L./Graves, Samuel B./Case, Randolph H. (1999): Formulating R&D Portfolios that Account for Risk. In: Research Technology Management, Vol. 42, No. 6, p. 40-43.

Rzasa, Philip V./Faulkner, Terrence W./Sousa, Nancy L. (1990): Analyzing R&D Portfolios At Eastman Kodak. In: Research Technology Management, Vol. 33, No. 1, p. 27-32.

Saaty, Thomas L. (1980): The Analytical Hierarchy Process. McGraw-Hill.

Scheinberg, Mark/Stretton, Alan (1994): Multiproject planning: tuning portfolio indices. In: International Journal of Project Management, Vol. 12, No. 2, p. 107-114.

Schmidt, Robert L./Freeland, James R. (1992): Recent Progress in Modeling R&D Project-Selection Processes. In: IEEE Transactions on Engineering Management, Vol. 39, No. 2, p. 189-201.

Schmidt, Jeffrey B./Calantone, Roger J. (1998): Are Really New Product Development Projects Harder to Shut Down? In: Journal of Product Innovation Management, Vol. 15, p. 111-123.

Shenhar, Aaron J. (1993): From low- to high-tech project management. In: R&D Management, Vol. 23, No. 3, p. 199-214.

Shenhar, Aaron J./Dvir, Dov (1995): Towards a typological theory of project management. In: Research Policy, Vol. 25, p. 607-632.

Shenhar, Aaron J. (2001): One Size Does Not Fit All Projects: Exploring Classical Contingency Domains. In: Management Science, Vol. 47, No. 3, p. 394-414.

Shenhar, Aaron J./Dvir, Dov/Levy, Ofer/Maltz, Alan C. (2001): Project Success: A Multidimensional Strategic Concept. In: Long Range Planning, Vol. 34, p. 699-725.

Söderlund, Jonas (2002): Managing complex development projects: arenas, knowledge process and time. In: R&D Management, Vol. 32, No. 5, p. 419-430.

Song, X. Michael/Parry, Mark E. (1996): What Separates Japanese New Product Winners from Losers. In: Journal of Product Innovation Management, Vol. 13, p. 422-439.

Souder, William E. (1973): Analytical Effectiveness of Mathematical Models for R&D Project Selection. In: Management Science, Vol. 19, No. 8, p. 907-923.

Souder, William E./Mandakovic, Tomislav (1986): R&D Project Selection Models. In: Research Management, Vol. 29, p. 36-42.

Souder, William E./Song, X. Michael (1997): Contingent Product Design and Marketing Strategies Influencing New Product Success and Failure in U.S. and Japanese Electronics Firms. In: Journal of Product Innovation Management, Vol. 14, No. 1, p. 21-34.

Terwiesch, Christian/Loch, Christoph/Niederkofler, Martin (1998): When Product Development Performance Makes a Difference: A Statistical Analysis in the Electronics Industry. In: Journal of Product Innovation Management, Vol. 15, p. 3-15.

The Economist (2007): The rise and fall of corporate R&D. Issue of March 3rd 2007, p. 69-71.

Thiry, Michel (2002): Combining value and project management into an effective programme management model. In: International Journal of Project Management, Vol. 20, p. 221-227.

Tuominen, Markku/Piippo, Petteri/Ichimura, Takaya/Matsumoto, Yoshio (1999): An analysis of innovation management systems' characteristics. In: International Journal of Production Economics, Vol. 60-61, p. 135-143.

Turner, J. R./Speiser, A. (1992): Programme management and its information systems requirements. In: International Journal of Project Management, Vol. 10, No. 4, p. 196-206.

Van Der Merwe, A. P. (1997): Multi-project management—organizational structure and control. In: International Journal of Project Management, Vol. 15, No. 4, p. 223-233.

Van Der Merwe, A. P. (2002): Project management and business development: integrating strategy, structure, processes and projects. In: International Journal of Project Management, Vol. 20, p. 401-411.

Wheelwright, Steven C./Sasser Jr., W. Earl (1989): The New Product Development Map. In: Harvard Business Review, May-June 1989, p. 112-125.

Wheelwright, Steven C./Clark, Kim B. (1992): Creating Project Plans to Focus Product Development. In: Harvard Business Review, March-April 1992, p. 70-82.

Wikipedia (2007): Analytic Hierarchy Process.
http://en.wikipedia.org/wiki/Analytic_Hierarchy_Process and http://de.wikipedia.org/wiki/Analytic_Hierarchy_Process, 1 October 2007.

Wiley, Victor D./Deckro, Richard F./Jackson Jr., Jack A. (1998): Optimization analysis for design and planning of multi-project programs. In: European Journal of Operational Research, Vol. 107, p. 492-506.

Yang, Kum-Khiong/Sum, Chee-Chuong (1997): An evaluation of due date, resource allocation, project release, and activity scheduling rules in a multiproject environment. In: European Journal of Operational Research, Vol. 103, p. 139-154.

Yap, Chee Meng/Souder, William. E. (1994): Factors Influencing New Product Success and Failure in Small Entrepreneurial High-Technology Electronics Firms. In: Journal of Product Innovation Management, Vol. 11, p. 418-432.

Zirger, Billie Jo/Maidique, Modesto A. (1990): A Model of New Product Development: An Empirical Test. In: Management Science, Vol. 36, No. 7, p. 867-883.

VDM publishing house ltd.

Scientific Publishing House

offers

free of charge publication

of current academic research papers, Bachelor's Theses, Master's Theses, Dissertations or Scientific Monographs

If you have written a thesis which satisfies high content as well as formal demands, and you are interested in a remunerated publication of your work, please send an e-mail with some initial information about yourself and your work to *info@vdm-publishing-house.com*.

Our editorial office will get in touch with you shortly.

VDM Publishing House Ltd.
Meldrum Court 17.
Beau Bassin
Mauritius
www.vdm-publishing-house.com

VDM Verlag Dr. Müller · LAP LAMBERT Academic Publishing · SVH Südwestdeutscher Verlag für Hochschulschriften